Growing up on a Shropshire Farm

Growing up on a Shropshire Farm

by
Diane Jacks

Logaston Press

LOGASTON PRESS
Little Logaston Woonton Almeley
Herefordshire HR3 6QH
logastonpress.co.uk

First published by Logaston Press 2007
Copyright © Stephen Meyer 2007

ISBN 978 1904396 67 3

Typeset by Logaston Press
and printed in Great Britain by
Bell & Bain Ltd., Glasgow

*Front cover illustrations: Aldon, near Craven Arms,
and a young Diana Jacks with the cows*

*To Cuthbert W. Jacks (1900-1972)
and Esther M. Jacks (née Colley) (1904-85),
of Rorrington, Chirbury and Aldon, Onibury*

Contents

Acknowledgments

For help with the content of this book I wish to thank John Bishop, Josie Challenor, John Colley, Leonard Colley, Ted and Nan Colley, Peter Humphries, Rusty Pinches, Margaret Whittal and Margaret Wilkinson. For help with putting the book together I would like to thank Stephen Meyer, my husband; Lynda Wilcox, my friend, Johanna Schiller my friend and carer, Andy Johnson of Logaston Press and Sarah Ellison who helped with the typing. For looking after me as the writing came together I must especially thank Stephen Meyer, Lynda Wilcox and Johanna Schiller, together with the doctors, nurses and physio and other therapists mostly based in Bishop's Castle.

To the hospital staff in Shrewsbury and (especially) Birmingham goes the credit for showing me that my discomfort, embarrassment and time is of no importance, and for teaching me what my childhood home had never succeeded in teaching me: how to lie and how to break a promise.

To all the friends, relations and neighbours who have supported us over the difficult time since 2003 — Thank you.

Preface

Memory is interwoven and interleaved, changing seamlessly from one level to another as you inspect it. In thinking about this subject, I have not only been thinking about my own memories, but about memories of memories. I have tried to make my parents' memories, at least of their adult years, as real to me as my own memories. I can't tell how far I have succeeded in what I have written, but I have succeeded inside my own head.

My father's diaries have given great assistance in sorting out this wash of recollections. They cover the period 1931 to 1971 with the exceptions of 1932, 1934 and 1937, for which the diaries are missing. They form the backbone of the parts of the book about Rorrington, they and my own memories that of the parts about Aldon, where I lived from my birth in 1943 until I went to university at 18. The first chapter about Stockton is essentially compiled from notes made by my mother in the 1970s.

The hero and heroine of this story are my father and mother, CW and EM Jacks. I use their first names, Cuth and Esther, in the chapters where they are children. When they married and he started to keep his diaries, I use their initials, CWJ and EMJ, which he usually used in the early decades.

He was ambitious, hard-working, gentle and generous. She was cool-headed, clear-sighted, peace-loving, independent and fair-minded. Born in the decade before 1910, they had roots in Victorian farming and cottage life and carried a range of the skills which had contributed to their families' self-sufficiency. They started farming in the 1930s and moved to a bigger farm in 1939, working right through the Second World War and the subsequent austerity of the 1950s, till the 1960s brought increasing prosperity, They managed to prosper in hard times, and take on new methods and prosper as times got better. No wonder I thought (as John Lennon later wrote) 'It's getting better all the time' as I grew up in the 1940s and '50s.

Because books without dates have always infuriated me, here are some key dates:

CWJ lived from   1900 to 1972
EMJ lived from   1904 to 1985
They were married in 1930 at Chirbury

Their first home together was at Rorrington, Chirbury, between 1930 and 1939. In 1939 they moved to Aldon, Craven Arms, where they lived till 1968. I, their only child, was born in 1943. In 1968 they moved to Church Stretton where they lived until CWJ died in 1972. They also had a seaside bungalow at Aberdovey. EMJ then moved to a bungalow in Montgomery, and lived there till her final illness and death in 1985.

My parents always tried to make me feel one of the family, but were careful to put no pressure on me to take on the farm. At first, in the '70s, I thought this was a mistake. Later, I was sure it was not. My job, in their eyes, was to do well at school and at university. I have tried to work hard — and now that I am told I have a brain tumour and no further treatment is possible, I have worked hard to get this material ready. We just don't know whether my life will now be measured in weeks, months, or years, my darling husband, Stephen, who looks after me so well, and I (his name is Stephen Meyer; mine, which I kept when we married, is Diane Jacks. Jacks is a good old Welsh border name and I felt I would like to keep it.)

Edgton
Craven Arms
June 2005

Diane collapsed and died in June 2005. Lynda Wilcox and I did our best to edit what Diane wrote, with subsequent help from Andy Johnson of Logaston Press. If you would like to read the original notes, ring me on 01588 680535.

Stephen Meyer,
Edgton,
Craven Arms
March 2006

Introduction

This book is written in and about south-west Shropshire, the hilly corner which lies next to the Welsh border and west of the A49. It is deep inland for Britain, so can be wet and cold. The low land is about 600 feet above sea level, and the low hills rise to 1,000 ft. It is very green and beautiful, and we love it very much. It has long been true that young people had to leave to make a living, and recently a lot of older people have second or retirement homes here.

Farming has been the main source of income in the county, but it has seen enormous changes over the last century. We can all read about Victorian high farming — high expenditure on input, for high returns, the slump in farming in the 1870s, and the slow, gradual recovery up to the First World War — but this is all rather too long ago for family memories. The western side of the country is wetter and more hilly than the east, and more suited to pastoral than arable farming, so it survived the 1870s and later years rather better. The First World War brought prosperity to farmers and the following years bankruptcy to many, including my mother's father.

In the 1920s and 1930s it was fashionable for the Council to buy up farms, split them into smallholdings, build a modern house and buildings on each, and let them. Many can still be seen around here. By the 1950s, you could barely make a living on a smallholding, and a decently profitable family farm required from 200 to 300 acres. By the end of the century farms had been united to make bigger units, and the 'normal' size now is probably well over 400 acres for a family farm in the border areas, although it is not uncommon to hear of holdings of over 2,000 acres. Once, most farmers were tenants of small estates, as my parents were. Now they are owner-occupiers, following the national fashion for owner-occupation. Besides, it helps your capital appreciate.

In the 1950s, country cottages were falling into disrepair and collapsing. On the estate where we lived the roofs were removed

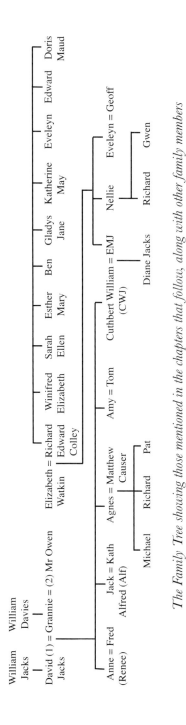

The Family Tree showing those mentioned in the chapters that follow, along with other family members

from many to prevent occupation by squatters. This seemed hard but was actually sensible. The cottages were tiny, often with just one enclosed bedroom along with another sleeping area on the landing. There was no water, no sanitation and access might be by half a mile or more of footpaths on shocking gradients, to say nothing of damp and other problems. But the tumbledown ruins made terrific places for us children to play and the danger of breaking in and going upstairs to walk on dodgy floorboards only gave added spice to the whole adventure.

In later years the cottages have been sold to incomers, who are doing them up, or roughly repaired for letting to holiday-makers as farmers frantically scramble for alternative sources of income, or used by the farmer's widow as planning regulations make it harder for her to build a smart new bungalow.

Once, the man was the farmer and his spouse 'the farmer's wife', as my mother's parents were. The farmer's wife may have been undervalued if she, like my grandmother, managed the house and the housework, the dairy with its constant round of milk-separating, butter and cheese-making, cleaning and scouring, and saw to the preparation of three hot and two cold

1. Elizabeth, 2. Nellie, 3. Esther, 4. Ben, 5. Gladys, 6. Katie, 7. Evelyn,
8. Edward, 9. Doris

meals a day for around twenty people, besides the baking of all the bread, cakes and pies.

Later, the couple became farmers, as my parents were (slightly ahead of time in the '40s). But my father said in his 1939 diary that the landlord has chosen 'us', not 'me', as the new tenant. In the 1950s they were business partners, and everything came addressed to 'Messrs CW and EM Jacks'.

'When a farm-man's wages were 30 shillings a week ...' — all my life EMJ would use this as a yardstick for various pieces of comparison. She was the one who liked working things out and so it was very useful to her, and it has been useful to me, although it referred to that slightly unreal time, the '30s. Then, as I understood it, a farm-man would earn his 30 shillings cash. He would also get his cottage rent free, a good garden, and a place to keep a pig. In addition there would be a row of potatoes in one of his employer's fields, and a reasonable amount of milk every day from the dairy.

I would rather not see set-aside, or fields and hills crammed with sheep. The scale and ugliness of many modern farm buildings is to be regretted. Yet there is still a very real farming community underlying the new developments. I have a great respect for the modern farmer's wife — having produced the children, she is equally at home with housework, cooking, gardening, e-mailing her far-flung family, travelling the world, driving one of the new big tractors, lambing the ewes, running the WI, and being a Councillor or a Churchwarden. I couldn't have done all that. Some of the changes are due to late twentieth-century feminism, some to her predecessors' lives.

My mother didn't get the vote until 1929, when she was 25 and married. She and my father both came from large families (nine and seven children respectively) and both disliked it (she particularly). For themselves, they planned a small family. Life for him had centred round his mother, when she and his grandfather kept the home going after his father's early death. EMJ's farmer father went bankrupt after the First World War and she had to leave school and be an untrained teacher. EMJ's dearly loved mother died in 1937. But EMJ knew what she wanted before then. She wanted to be with her husband, and if that meant working alongside him outside (then not generally done by women) that is what she would do. So, on their tiny hill farm, where the harvest was of hay, she pitched to him as he stood on the loose hay (or fell off — he was always in such a hurry that he often had falls and accidents). Sixty-three times they loaded and roped the dray one year, after which the horse could draw it to the building or to the stack, where CWJ would thatch it. She also did her share of the hand-milking, made butter, reared and dressed poultry and helped to run the shop. At lambing time or when a cow was calving he got up even earlier than his normal 5.30am, and she stayed up till the middle of the night. I couldn't have done that either.

CHAPTER ONE
Stockton 1910-1918

My maternal grandmother Elizabeth Colley (née Watkin) had been to a private school — her father wouldn't let her go to the local village school because the girls had to clean it. She was smart and well-dressed — the kind of person who demanded respect. She was also good and kind, and I don't recall her ever losing her temper.

Grandfather was very generous, free and easy; he'd give anything away, whether or not the beneficiary could pay for it. He had a snakeskin; he said he'd killed the snake with a whip from horseback. Perhaps he had. He and his brother Ben had gone to Australia in the 1890s because there was no work for them on the small family hill farm in Wales. Then their parents moved to Wilmington and could give them work, so they came home. Ben died in England in the early 1920s. Grandfather had a beautiful voice — part-singing (where three or more voices are required) from his Welsh background, it was worth going to church to hear him. Most of the rest of the family could hardly sing in tune.

My grandfather was one of nine children: Winifred Elizabeth, Sarah Ellen, Esther Mary, Ben, Katherine May, Evelyn Anne, Richard Edward (my grandfather), Gladys Jane, and Doris Maud. Ben died in the 'flu epidemic after the First World War. Before that, as a young child, he'd had polio which left him with one leg shorter than the other. Mother used to take him to see the orthopaedic surgeon, Sir Robert Jones, in Birkenhead. Edward had meningitis as a child. To treat him they got ice from the icehouse at Powys Castle, and put it on his head in a rubber bag. Katy had epileptic fits; once she swung round a kettle of boiling water as the fit came on her, scalding those around.

No one really understood the illness then, and it gradually changed her from the bright little girl she had been. Esther once had pneumonia, and was nursed night and day downstairs in the parlour. She said that at one stage everything had seemed to go very dark and she thought she was surely dead.

Nellie (Sarah Ellen) was the favourite of grandmother's mother from Wilmington. This great-grandmother was a she-devil, but she was a hard worker. Her husband was very refined, and didn't work. Grandmother took her things to Shrewsbury to sell in the market; Welshpool was nearer, but it wasn't good enough for

*My maternal grandmother,
Elizabeth Colley*

her. Perhaps it was from her that a jealous, quarrelsome streak came into the family. Three of the sisters all took after her in that way. Nellie was also a good worker; Lizzie wasn't bad-tempered, but she could work all day and not do half what Nellie would; Esther worked hard initially as an assistant teacher and then on the farms.

The girls wore white pinafores with frills and yokes to go to school and dark pinafores at home. These dresses were made at home, but they were the best-dressed children around, except perhaps those from Marton Hall. Underneath the pinafores were starched petticoats, calico chemises and knickers, all frilled and flounced. They had liberty bodices and knitted stockings. In summer they had tussore silk dresses for best, and in winter they had tailor-made grey coats from the Royal Welsh Warehouse in Newtown, from cloth made in Newtown. They would be taken there to be measured and fitted.

My grandmother would drive to Forden and leave the trap at the station; Ellen, her older sister, would come in by train from her home at the Porth, near Moat Lane Junction, and they would shop together. The sisters were very fond of each other. Esther spent a lot of time at the Porth as a child — sent there for a bit of peace from Nellie, who bullied her. Shoes and boots were made and mended by the boot maker, William Jacks. They were waterproof, and they needed to be so near to the river; the cottage children always had wet feet in winter.

MARTON, CHIRBURY,

(Mid) _____ 190l

Mr _Colley_

Dr. to W. JACKS & SON,
Boot and Shoe Makers.

PAIRS NEATLY AND PROMPTLY ATTENDED TO.

Jan 6	Nelleys Boots repaired	.	.	8.
4	Girls Boots nailed round			6.
9	Benneys Boots repaired		1	
March 18	Nellies Boots repaired			8.
27	Nellies Boots Soled round 1 toecap		2	4.
30	Bennies Boots Soled round te		1	10
April 3	Elizabeth Boots Soled round		2	4.
10	Esters Boots Soled round		2	3
June 2?	Mr Boots nailed			6
		£	12	1

Paid July 17/11
E H Jacks

A bill from boot maker William Jacks paid by EHJ

3

Grandfather was Church but grandmother was Chapel, so the children went to both. In the morning, they went to church with grandfather, while grandmother saw to things at home. In the afternoon they went to the chapel Sunday School. The church ran a club into which people paid in a shilling a week, the Church then doubled it and they had enough money to go shopping once a year. Against this the Sunday school ran an annual trip to Aberystwyth. The carrier's horse and cart would be hired to take loads of children to Forden station.

The farm-workers' wives were never given a lift in grandfather's trap. If they didn't go to Welshpool in the carrier's cart, they could walk. One used to do very well at the market — there would be plenty of drunken farmers there! She'd push four or five children all the way — redheaded, black, fair — and stop by the roadside to suckle them.

If anyone was hurt in an accident and needed to go to hospital, they used to send for grandfather and Kitty, his pretty, high-stepping pony. He would take the trap, collect the victim and Kitty would go the 20 miles to the Royal Salop Infirmary in Shrewsbury as fast as possible — she was the fastest way of travelling in that long valley with no railway and no main road.

It was a big household, for apart from the parents and nine children, there were living-in men, and two maids who also lived in. Nellie Price was a maid who stayed for about 12 years, and her brother, Walter Price, lived in as well. Nellie Price was a good worker, and nice-looking too. She could cook as well as do the housework. There was a nursemaid as well — a girl of 14 to 16, who looked after the young children, keeping them from falling in the fire, and took them for a walk on Saturday afternoons so that everything could be tidy ready for Sunday. One of these nursemaids was Molly Owen, who had dark hair in plaits. It was her job to put the children to bed, and they used to insist that she looked under the bed to see that there was no devil there. Once she refused, and Nellie threw her slipper at her; the slipper missed the girl, broke the glass and went out through the window. The youngest children slept in their parents' room, the boys shared another room; the oldest girls shared one of the attic rooms, and the maids shared another. The living-in men slept in another attic bedroom. Baths were taken in the kitchen in front of the fire. The maids wore dark pinafores for their work, and the nursemaid had a white one to go out on the road when the children were taken for walks.

Collecting postcards was fashionable in those days, and when Nellie Price went on holiday she would send Esther a postcard. This used to earn her a beating from one of her jealous sisters.

The men would live in for perhaps two years, and then move on. There were always three or four of them. They would get up at 6am, and feed and water the horses and cattle. Breakfast was taken at 7am — broth with bread, bread and cheese, and cider or tea. (It was a huge job to feed the men well, and it was said that at Hockleton and Llewynrhedydd they only got broth, and that was often stinking.) The next meal was bait, at 10 or 11am. For most of the men this would consist of cold bread and bacon, or bread and cheese, washed down with bottles of beer or cider, which they would have outside. The cowman, who worked near the house, would come in for his meal. Dinner would be the same as the family had — meat and vegetables, followed by pudding. The meat might be beef, lamb, rabbits — or pork when a pig had been killed. At Christmas and Michaelmas, and sometimes on Sundays, there would be a goose, two ducks, two chickens, or pheasants. Everything was cooked with the proper stuffings and other accompaniments — pork with apple sauce, beef with horseradish, rabbits, pheasants and chickens stuffed with forcemeat or sage and onions, and covered with bacon. Hares were cooked in cream.

On school days, the children had dinner at 5pm when they came home, on other days they had the same tea as the men. The men had their tea at 7pm when they finished work (though they might still have to attend to the horses afterwards). There would be bread and cheese, bread and jam, cake and fruit pie. There was no helping yourself from the jam dish — it was a spoonful of jam put on your plate and make it last. There was always beer and cider for the men, whenever they wanted. The men who didn't live in would get their meals at harvest time — harvest was hard work, and they couldn't work hard enough on the food they had at home.

At Stockton, the men had their meals in the back kitchen, and the maids had theirs in the kitchen with the family, but at a separate table. In most places the maids ate with the men, but grandmother wouldn't allow that. Farmhouse maids had a bad reputation, but none of hers 'got into trouble'.

The men went up to their attic bedroom through the scullery. In the evenings they would sit out in the stable playing cards, playing the mouth organ, or listening to Walter Price's gramophone. On winter evenings, when it became too dark for them to work in the fields, they would saw wood and do other odd jobs.

There was half an acre of vegetable garden, and great-uncle Evan Watkin looked after that. He lived nearby at Rhyd-y-Groes, but his wife had left him, and he came to Stockton for all his meals. He caught moles, skinned them, dried the skins and sold them by post. It was a great business for the children to help him to pack and post off the skins. He also caught rabbits both at Stockton and on other relations' farms. He never poached pheasants — unless one happened to get in a rabbit wire! The men didn't get any of the game. There was also wild duck; that was poached too. Father was a grand shot down by the river.

Evan was one of those people who can do everything well, and the garden was a picture. There were new potatoes (main crop potatoes and swedes were grown in the fields), onions, shallots, carrots, beet-root, rows and rows of peas and beans, and all the different cabbages in season, but no parsnips because grandmother didn't like them. There was plenty of manure to make everything grow well. For herbs there was thyme, parsley, sage and mint. The only bought vegetables we had were packets of dried peas for a treat, on Sundays in winter. There were currants — red, white and black, gooseberries, raspber-ries, apples, plums, pears, damsons and cider apples.

To make the cider, all the apples would be gathered up in heaps including bad apples and dirt. A horse would walk round and round the jinney ring to drive the presses which pulped the apples, and the men would carry the juice, two buckets at a time, down the outside steps to the cellar.

Labour was cheap, and things were carried on men's backs — often no-one bothered to load a cart. All the swedes and mangolds were pulped by hand, straw was chopped and oats rolled, although later there were oil engines. Straw was cut on the jinney ring, and wheat and barley were taken to the mill to be ground.

The horses were important, although they weren't pure-bred Shires, like they had at Wilmington. The head waggoner in charge of the horses was called Ned Abberley, and lived in a farm cottage. This was an important job, and he was a clever man who could have gone far if he had had the right opportunity. He had one skill which delighted the children: he could whistle beautifully. He was well-known round about because of this, and won a lot of competitions. The under-waggoner was one of the men who lived in. The cowman lived out, and there were two or three other general workmen. One of these was Wally Price, Nellie Price's brother. He fought in the First World War and was killed right at the end. Part of the rent for the farm at Wilmington was carting the coal from Forden station to Gunley Hall — a job that the men did on wet days in winter.

There was plenty of work to do in the house as well. Cooking for the family, men and maids — about twenty people every day — and washing up. Grandfather would light the fires in the morning — it was no trouble to him to get up. There was the boiler, the kitchen fire and the back kitchen fire. The grate in the front kitchen was black-leaded every day, and the stone flagged floors in the kitchen and the back kitchen washed. The front kitchen had tiles and rugs by the fireplace. Then there were the beds to be made and the bedrooms had to be swept and dusted — feather-beds made so much dust.

In the dairy the milk would go into the separator, and one of the younger men turned the handle for half an hour or more. The skim milk was fed to the calves, and cream was made into butter. Because there wasn't much milk in winter, big steins of very salty butter were put down in summer to last through the barren months. The separator had to be scoured and the buckets and strainer boiled in the boiler every day. Churning was done once a week for most of the year, and twice a week in summer. The dairy was cleaned every day, and once a week all the slabs were moved and cleaned. Later on a creamery started up nearby to which milk was sold.

Each day had its special jobs as well. Monday was washing day. Mrs Griffiths came from 9am to 4pm, and she and Nellie Price did the washing, with help from the other maid. They had to leave off to get dinner, which would be cold meat with vegetables. Nellie Price and Mrs Griffiths used two tubs, one with a ridged board to rub the rough things. Only sheets were washed for the men who lived in — they either sent their clothes home, or got some woman in the village to take in their other washing. Sheets, tablecloths and other white items were boiled in the boiler with washing powder, and then blued and starched. There was a mangle to wring out sheets and large things. It was hard work for two people, one to turn the handle and one to catch the sheet as it came out. If the weather was bad the washing was put on massive clothes-horses and left in the kitchen at night to dry. The sheets weren't ironed; they were folded, damped and put through the mangle. Then there was everything else to sprinkle and iron — hours and hours of it, heating the flat irons in front of a red hot fire in the kitchen range. There was a stand which hooked in front of the fire to hold the irons up to the heat. It was hot work, so in summer it would be done in the evening. Blankets and bedspreads were washed on very hot dry days in summer, and put through the mangle.

Monday was also market day in Welshpool, to which grandmother went. Market clothes were second-best. Kitty, the pretty pony, would pull the big trap. Depending on the time of year, there was butter packed in huge side-baskets, eggs to sell at sixpence a score, cheese, chickens, rabbits, gooseberries, currants, apples and pears. She would set out at 10.30am and get back at 4pm. When she'd unloaded at the market hall, dealers would buy chickens, ducks, and rabbits. With the rest she would sit at one of the long wooden tables while people bought. At the end of the day the dealers bought up everything that was left — cheaply, of course.

Grandmother also did her shopping on market day. She took the order to the grocer, and the grocer took some butter to sell in his shop. Later in the day, she went back to pick up the groceries. It was a treat to go to market with her, and when the children went, it was strictly in turn. In that family of squabbling children, there were turns for everything, even scraping a pudding dish. They would take their own butter, and go into a restaurant for a pot of tea and penny buns; then spread their own butter on the buns. Grandmother bought yeast in Welshpool, and coffee, which she loved. She also bought half a pound of custard creams, to be eaten before bed on Sundays, and a Battenberg cake; the children had some to take to school for dinner on Tuesday.

Lots of people shopped at the Spar because it was cheap. There were bits of stone in the dried fruit. Even the well-to-do family from the Porth shopped at the Spar.

Horses for sale were taken to market in Welshpool, but cattle went to Montgomery where the auction was held on Broad Street. The dealers were mostly rogues, but one, Johnny Evans, was as fair as he could be; he bought a lot of stock direct from farms and never rogued anybody. He would even help farmers who were struggling — he'd supply them with stock to graze, and pay for the improvement the animals made while they were on the farms. He thought the world of grandmother, and in later years, whenever he met one of the children, he would say 'What a wonderful woman your mother was'. Once he gave the children a black heifer, so that they would have whatever money it made when it was sold.

When the First World War came, everything flourished and there was plenty of money to be made, even though many items, such as traction engines, were requisitioned by the government. Shepherds, the fair people, had a contract to fell woods near Stockton, using their big steam engines to haul timber, instead of fairground equipment. They bought nearly all the food the farms could sell, and paid more than the market. The women were smart, with their hair in curls, and the men were fine smart chaps, many of them six-footers. Round Wotherton the ground was riddled with old spar mines, and the family used to be afraid that their caravans and the bright, beautiful traction engines would fall into the old shafts — but they didn't. The timber carriages were huge, and they cut up the roads dreadfully, making ruts two feet deep. However, the war was the making of farming in that part of the country — but afterwards came the slump.

Baking was done on Friday. It started as soon as breakfast was over. The flour was put in the bread mit — a big wooden box which was also used to store bread once it was baked. The yeast was put with sugar and water to prove, then put into the flour with more water to mix the dough. The dough was kneaded, allowed to rise, and made into loaves. Meanwhile, the baking oven would have been heated. After the last baking, sticks would have been put in the oven to dry. They were taken out and a fire started in the mouth of the oven with small dry sticks and fire from the grate. When it was burning, more sticks were added and it was pushed right into the oven. You could tell when the oven was hot enough because the stones round the mouth would go white hot. The ashes were raked out, and the oven washed with a bag tied on the end of a stick until it was really clean. Then the bread was slid in on a flat piece of metal on the end of a long stick. The bread went right into the end of the oven, and pies and cakes for the week went nearer the mouth because they didn't take so long to cook.

Sometimes the family had to buy flour, but mostly we took our own corn to Cilcwydd to the water mill. In the war we had an oil engine which was used to grind corn for the cattle. It was illegal to use it to make flour because of rationing.

The bread was beautiful when it was hot — so it went quicker! Great-grandmother baked bread each week (with their own flour), but no-one was allowed to eat it until it was a week old. It could then be cut thinner, and no-one wanted so much, but if left too long it went mouldy, when the men wouldn't eat it. Great-grandfather used to cut very fine brown bread and butter and sprinkle it with sugar for the children — behind Grandmother's back. Grandmother made cream cheese to sell to the halls and big houses.

Water came from a spring in the big field, and was piped to the well. The men would pump water to fill the big boiler, and then anyone would get a bucket of water to use in the kitchen. There was a pool in the farmyard, also fed from the spring, where the animals would drink. Stockton mill was disused by this time, although it still stood on the Camlad. There was a bridge over the river, and a footpath which the children used to go to school. The river was cutting away the bank, and there were often floods, so that sometimes they had to go to school by the road; on those days they took the pony and trap, which dropped them at the pub in the village. At least there was always water for the stock; on many farms there were fields which couldn't be used for stock because there was no water.

The children went to the Church of England school in Chirbury, starting before they were five years old. They should really have gone to school in Marton,

Granny and Esther

10

Lizzie and Esther

because it was nearer, but Marton had schoolmistresses who didn't keep very good order, and Chirbury had a schoolmaster, Mr Shaw, who was noted for learning and discipline. Mrs Shaw also taught, and there was another teacher called Miss Watkin. There were about 140 children on the register. The school day ran from 9.30am to 4pm, and started with prayers and a hymn, the calling of the register, and then half an hour of current affairs. Mr Shaw was an important person in the village — being also choirmaster and organist.

The children from Stockton walked two miles to school. They took their lunch with them, and at first they would leave it in the school cloakroom. But other children soon got to know who had good lunches, with something tasty to go with the bread, and sometimes they would help themselves. So after a time it was arranged that the family's children should take their lunch to one of the cottages and go there to eat it at the mid-day break.

Esther was evidently a bright child, and was rather a favourite with the Shaws. Eventually she went to the County High School for Girls in Welshpool, either cycling to the station at Forden, or cycling all the way to Welshpool. She loved the High School, especially the games. She was good at tennis, and also played hockey for the school which often involved travelling to other towns on a Saturday. She would have liked to stay on at school and train as a games mistress, but money was too tight at home to allow it.

Grandfather went bankrupt in the 1920s — a lot of farmers did after the First World War. The family moved to a smallholding in Worthen, a neighbouring parish, with Lizzie officially as tenant, and later in her life an active small farmer. Nellie went to Shrewsbury to train as a nurse, and Esther left school to work as an assistant teacher in the village school with Mr and Mrs Shaw. Grandmother died in 1937, grandfather in the early 1950s.

CHAPTER TWO

Wotherton and my father's family

When young I remember hearing about 'Grandad' William Jacks, in fact my father's grandfather. My father was only a little boy when his own father died.

Born in 1836, Grandad was lame. I think he had a club foot, but I'm not sure. When he was a boy, they lived at Middleton, and his mother used to borrow a donkey to take him to the Royal Salop Infirmary in Shrewsbury. He rode, and she walked the nearly 20 miles each way.

'Grannie' was my actual grandmother, having married my grandfather, David Jacks, who died before the First World War. David had a drink problem and they lived too near the pub. He was reported to have been seen taking coppers from the children's money boxes to buy a drink. After he died, the family was kept together by Grannie and my father's two grandfathers — Grandad, the lame cobbler, and William Davies, who was a foreman at Wotherton mine. The family moved from Marton, where they had lived in Holmwood House, to 32 Wotherton, where they had a good cottage on the Wakeman estate until the 1970s.

Sir Offley Wakeman was a much-loved landlord. He had been injured in the First World War, and had a small silver plate on his skull where he had been wounded. In the 1930s he found work in his woods for unemployed men, so the Rorrington estate brought him little income. When Grannie was in her 80s, her greatest treat was when he came in his little car and took her to church. The difference in class mattered less with age and the passing of time, and people had always found him easy to talk to.

In the very early years of motor cars, two which were often seen were Sir Offley's, with its Shropshire AW registration, and the Earl of Powis's, bearing Montgomeryshire's EP. The boys worked out that EP stood for 'Earl of Powis' and AW for 'Awfly Wakeman'.

A good cottage, like 32 Wotherton, was still the same in the 1940s and 1950s, when I remember it. You went through the wicket and up the garden path, with a lawn and flowers to one side, a huge vegetable garden decently screened off by a hedge on the other, and in through the back door, which Grannie always kept open (ajar even in winter), straight into the kitchen. Outside the kitchen door was a patch of cement, a dry and level surface for odd jobs and extra room for washing days when the mangle would be brought out there. Inside there was no electricity (but who had electricity in the country then?), a sink with cold running water, but no hot, a huge black-leaded fireplace with an oven and a fire, however small, always burning, so that there was hot water in the kettle and a fire for cooking. You raised the oven temperature by building up the fire. On the mantelpiece were two red-and-white china dogs. The floor was of red tiles, with a rug in front of the fireplace, and the two comfortable chairs in front of the fire were wooden Windsor-type armchairs with cushions and rugs. There were wooden chairs round the kitchen table, where we ate, a small rocking chair much loved by all the children in turn, and a hard sofa between the wall and the table for children, who reached it by crawling under the table. The mangle stood snugly against one wall.

Later, once electricity had arrived, the sink had a hot-water tap as well, there was an electric cooker, an upholstered chair for Grannie, and the mangle went outside. Simple comforts indeed, but people used to say that, in the 1950s, with the old-age pension and a small contribution from the only son still at home, she was better off than she'd ever been. For a long time one of my cousins lived there with her daughter, and did a lot of the work.

There used to be one mine at Wotherton and more at the Grit and Snailbeach. That at Wotherton produced spar, of which there was a large piece on Grannie's kitchen window-sill — white and sparkling, with lots of ridges which could have trapped dust. Yet it was always clean — there was never any dust.

Through the kitchen you reached the 'front kitchen', or what might now be called the dining room — a cold, smart room with tables and chairs and the best furniture, a lamp on the centre of the table before electricity came, and a photograph of my long-dead grandfather. Grandad's desk was there, along with a grandfather clock. I never saw this front room used. The front door also opened into this room from a large porch, and an internal door opened into a lobby, which led to the larder, a cool stone room down two steps. The staircase went up from the lobby. I never knew the upstairs, but I believe there were three bedrooms. It was crowded, and people had to sleep on the floor if necessary. As years went by, there were fewer people and less pressure on bed spaces.

The lavatory, naturally, was down the garden, next to 'the shop' or the cobbler's workshop, with neat squares of newspaper hung up behind the door.

Five children resulted from Grannie's marriage with David Jacks: Irene Annie (Renee), Cuthbert William (my father, Cuth, born in 1900, and called after one of the gentlemen in a smart house where Grannie had worked), Jack Alfred (Alf), Agnes, and Amy. Grannie married a second time, presumably hoping for better luck, but her second choice wasn't much better, although he fathered two sons, Dennis and Walter. Remembering that one of them was born only a few days before Christmas, my mother once said 'They wouldn't have had much of a Christmas that year, with Renee in charge — no! Renee would have been at work! With poor little Ag trying to look after everything at only seven or eight.' They were poor and

Irene in 1915

had hardly enough to eat. 'Mock duck' said my mother. 'If they had a marrow stuffed with sage and onions and roasted in the oven, that would be marvellous.'

Cuth referred to himself as CWJ and his wife — my mother — as EMJ in his diaries, and this is how I will refer to them. CWJ's step-father died in 1937. CWJ was the only person I knew with a brother, half-brothers, and step-brothers, although I grew up without knowing the step-brothers. They were Ernest and Harry Owen, and Harry used to come on a little motor-bike to Sunday tea. He was killed in the First World War.

CWJ was the oldest boy in the family of five by his own father, and was given responsibility for many day-to-day tasks. Once the little ones could say 'th', they had to call him 'Cuth', not 'Cuff'. As he grew older, he had to leave school and go to work; to go as a soldier; to help Grandad and learn to be a cobbler; to find some work for his step-father and younger half-brothers during the later years at Rorrington; to write the business letters and to take the lead on many occasions.

It was at Marton that CWJ first went to school, then later in Chirbury. All the big boys from Marton went there because there was a master to keep them in order. Mr Shaw at Chirbury happened to be one of those inspirational teachers who are remembered for years. My father learned *The Ballad of the Revenge*, *We are Seven*, *I Remember, I Remember, the House where I was Born* and other popular poems. Mr Shaw also seems to have taught them scripture and a rousing sort of patriotic history. Mr Shaw had been to Cheltenham College of Education, was keen on sport, and he and Mrs Shaw evidently had wider horizons than most of the local people as they used to go on cycling holidays to France.

My father's birthday was in August, so he was able to leave school at the age of 11 in 1911 after passing Standard IV. He got a job as 'boy' in the post office in Worthen, where Mrs Lloyd was kind to him. Later he worked at the Aldress farm near Churchstoke where they called him 'Bill'. He was bitterly homesick in both places, and learned streams of Welsh verbatim from the other farm-workers, without understanding it at all. Presumably they were homesick for Wales. Then he went back home to help Grandad with the cobbler's business, and keep a few pigs.

As the boys got older and the girls went out into service, the mile or so to Chirbury seemed no distance, and the boys joined in village life, games and entertainments.

CWJ loved church, especially coming out of the dark into the high, light, airy space for the working-class Evensong. (Those who worked for others would have jobs to do at home on Sunday morning and would go to the evening service after the work was done. Those who had people to work for them would usually go to church in the morning.) He loved the music (hymns are simple enough even for the non-musical, and you can ignore one psalm per evening, or concentrate on the words). And all those wonderful words — magic, especially once he had left school and poetry behind him. People did go readily to the pictures in Welshpool, but the traditional village 'entertainment' was church with its music.

At one time Cuth played football for Chirbury. The team wasn't very good, and in one match was soundly beaten by the opponents. Not giving up, the team wrote a splendid report afterwards about the excellent play, in attack or defence, of each member, and rushed it to the newspaper office. The system seemed to be that the first report to be received got printed, so this did. The actual score, defeat by something like 20-1, appeared extraordinary after the excellent play of Chirbury, and the team-members were pleased with themselves.

Life was hard for many, and drink and disease made it harder. Children from poor-quality houses used to go to school with the marks on their ears where the rats had bitten them in the night. A whole family of young people could be wiped out by TB, because the carer was so often the next to be stricken. Some families were poorer than others because the father drank (and probably also hit his wife and children).

Most women didn't drink, or at least not much. One older woman who did drink would arrive at the pub in her little car; there was no driving test then, and no breath test. When it was time for her to go, the men would all stream out after her and PUSH her car round to face home. She had never learnt to reverse. People discovered there had been some advantages to horses. The man staggering out of the pub could collapse into a trap, tell the pony to go home, and take no more notice. He couldn't do that with a car.

One old man who lived in the hills came down occasionally to the village to do his shopping. A lot of people laughed once when he came down on a Sunday by mistake. The people in the village knew they were more sophisticated than the people living in the mining villages or in isolated cottages in the hills. So there was more laughter when one man from the hills said 'our owd wenches' (his two daughters) were so smart now they had gone into service that they had told him 'to build a proper shit-house'.

Meanwhile the First World War was at last nearing its end. In August 1918 Cuth was called up, whisked through a brief training,

Studio photographs of CMJ when caled up with, on the right, his grandfather and either Dennis or Walter

CWJ is second from left in the middle row

CWJ is second from left in the back row

some of which stuck for life, and given anti-smallpox jabs. He was assigned to the Transport Corps, presumably because he already knew something about motorbikes. The conscripts had to learn a list of items to go in the kit-bag — he could still remember it in the '50s. In November 1918 he was at Hastings waiting for transport to France. Fortunately, the Armistice came first. He always used to say that the Kaiser had to surrender 'once he knew I was coming'.

Back at home, he worked with Grandad, did the garden, kept a few more pigs, and bought a motor-bike. He preferred the gardening to working indoors cobbling. The pigs did well, and in the 1930s (and probably earlier) he rented some land at the Folly to enable him to keep a few more animals. It was a lifestyle still followed by youngest half-brother, Walter, in the '50s, then well into middle age, renting a few fields and living 'at home' with the garden, the motor-bike, the pigs, and the evenings out.

CWJ was an unusually tall, well-built chap at six feet, even taller than his younger brother, Alf, who was very like him. The three girls had sandy hair and were incredibly frail, being both tiny and slight. Only Amy, the youngest sister, was a reasonable height whilst Renee, the eldest, was the smallest. Perhaps the whole business of taller boys and slighter girls harked back to Victorian days of insufficient food for

19

*CWJ sharing his love of motorbikes
with Granny*

the poor, when the women went without to keep the men fit to work.

During the 1930s, Grannie was fortunate enough to see all her children, not just Cuth, working in reasonable jobs. Renee was in service, at first in a big parsonage, later in high-class houses all over the British Isles. She married a veteran of the First World War who was also in service. Alf was a mechanic at George Parry's garage at Forden as well as giving driving lessons. He was later to become a lorry-driver. Agnes was in service again, like Renee, in big

EMJ looking a little apprehensive ...

houses all over the country. After the Second World War she married a sergeant in the British Army of the Rhine and moved to Telford. Amy too was in service in big houses, but locally so that she could cycle home on days off. She was to marry a smallholder who also worked as a contractor with JCBs and diggers.

Dennis was a farmworker (starting on his half-brother's farm) who rose to become a farm manager and tenant farmer. Walter was also a farmworker (again, starting

... but is willing to try

From left to right: CMJ with EMJ, CMJ's younger brother, Alf, and an unknown friend or cousin

CMJ (standing) and his brother, Alf

with his half-brother), and later became one of a gang repairing roads. Unmarried, he lived 'at home' till he died.

The daughters who went into service seem to have been ambitious to work in big houses with a large staff, and Renee and Agnes both specialised in cookery.

With the arrival of electricity at no.32, and subsequently the television, Grannie started to watch, and love, the hymn-singing programme early on Sunday evenings.

Sometime afterwards the Wakeman Estate sent an architect round to draw up plans to install bathrooms and running water. As there was already running cold water, and the porch waiting to be converted to a downstairs bathroom, this proved not to be too difficult. Because Grannie always had the kitchen door open so she could see the road, we suggested she had a glass door fitted at the same time as that would not be so draughty. This didn't go down at all well; she hung a lace curtain over it, and would have preferred the old way.

Meal-times were even more important before the coming of television. We always had a meal when we went to Grannie's, but usually only tea or supper. It was nearly always the same — a white table-cloth on the scrubbed table, bread, bread-board, bread-knife, butter and someone to cut the bread and arrange it on a big green-and-white bread-plate. There was a plate, knife and perhaps fork for everyone, depending on the food. Usually we had bread and butter and jam or Cheddar cheese and pickles. The jam was often gooseberry, which we never had at home, and the jam and pickles would be home-made, using garden produce. Then there would be a slice of cake — dripping cake, or home-made sponge, perhaps, and cups of tea. Walter would have his cooked dinner taken from the oven on a plate if he came in at this time. My young cousin and I would sit on the sofa behind the table, under the photograph of Aberystwyth with waves over the promenade. But we had to ask 'Please may I get down now?' when we had finished. I didn't have to do that at home, so I was never sure whether it applied to me (or was I too old by then?). When there were too many people for everyone to sit round the kitchen table to eat, children used to sit at the mangle. I saw my cousins do this, but there was always a place at the table for me. I suppose, after all, my father was the oldest son. After meals, children might, with permission, play at board-games or jig-saw puzzles on the table, or, in the light evenings, go outside and play.

Grannie always had aches and pains and used to rub her joints. On her left hand the ring finger was permanently set in a shut position following some accident. She also had a touch of gout — when we said 'But you have to be a rich man to have gout' she would laugh and say the doctor had said this was 'poor old lady's gout'. She wore old-fashioned clothes, all black, grey and purple, with perhaps a bit of white lace or net. This fascinated me in a way — my mother wore blues and greens and an occasional brown tweed. Sometimes Grannie used to come with us on holiday, when we went to visit her eldest daughter in the south.

When Grannie was frail towards the end of her life her daughters were summoned 'home' to nurse her and run the house for the youngest son who remained at home. Sons, and granddaughters, were allowed into the pantry for food and china to lay the table. My mother, as a daughter-in-law, was not allowed to do these things(!) but she was allowed to buy and cook the fish for lunch. In a similar vein, one of my cousins once offered to wash the kitchen floor, but his would not do for Grannie, who had to have her own daughter do it.

When the old lady was in her 90s and dying, when no-one wanted to nurse her at home in the old-fashioned way for more than a few days at a time (and who shall blame them?), my mother sat and held her hand for a long time, in what used to be the workhouse. They had their own lives, and Grannie had lived through more than one generation in ideas and habits, right into the 1960s.

CHAPTER THREE

Marriage & Rorrington

EMJ had a glorious time at the County School in Welshpool, and it was hard to give up her ambition to go to college and go to work when her father went bankrupt. But she did it, and after work teaching infants in the village school, she started unpicking and turning the younger girls' dresses, so they had something decent to go about in. She and her mother were not going to get into debt.

Chirbury Ladies Hockey: Hockey Shield Final at Brompton in 1923
Back row: Annie Jenkins, Ethel Evans, May Hollway
Middle row: Prudence Williams, Siss Williams, Esther Colley
Front row: Mrs Knowles, Winnie Cadwallader, Doris Jones, Sybil Knowles,
Siss Jerman

CMJ and EMJ's wedding.
EMJ wore a wedding-dress chosen from the best she could afford.
No white wedding for her — she wanted a dress that would be useful afterwards.
It was made of a kind of silk crepe in cafe-au-lait, with printed red and blue
flowers, and red binding round the flounces on the skirt and round the sash.
She did try to alter it later, but it was too difficult, so she left it

My father and mother were married in Chirbury church on 9 June 1930. His brother Alf was best man, and her sister Lizzie was bridesmaid. CWJ and EMJ had known each other as children at school. The years between them, which seemed nothing at 20, were a huge gap between 7 and 11. The 1920s were their play-time, their magic youth, in spite of being so grim for so many. They were an accepted couple at dances, concerts and whist drives in the village hall, taking holidays with

Above and lower left: Visiting Aberystwyth in August 1927

relations, and using his motor-bike for transport. She rode pillion, and he had a sidecar which could be removed. They had no housekeeping responsibilities, although she did a lot of dressmaking for her newly-poor sisters. For herself, she liked to buy the best she could afford.

At the time of their marriage mother was assistant mistress in Chirbury village school, teaching the infants, while Mr Richard Shaw was headmaster, and she continued in her job for a time after her

Chirbury School with EMJ in 1922 — her first year there?

marriage. It is interesting that Mr Winnington Ingram, the incumbent of Chirbury, who knew them both well, wrote on the marriage certificate that my father was a smallholder, and she, not schoolmistress, but daughter of a smallholder. In fact, her father was a bankrupt farmer, and the 'official' smallholder was the bridesmaid. Not much appreciation then of the position of women.

In spite of the dreadful condition of farming, my father had just rented from Sir Offley Wakeman a smallholding of 13.9 acres in Rorrington with hill grazing rights, and the village shop,

EMJ during the time she was teaching at Chirbury School

which they didn't particularly want, for £27 10s a year. But it was in their natures to do their best — whether at farming or shop-keeping.

After a honeymoon spent in Llandudno, they came home prepared to work hard to build up the farm. They were both from fairly large families, and neither liked it much. For themselves they wanted a much smaller family, when they had more time and money. So they bought a copy of Marie Stopes's *Married Love* and waited. Being among the oldest of their own families (he the second and she the third), they found it hard to see their siblings have families before them, when CWJ especially was so fond of children. It was a treat for those who lived nearby to visit Rorrington, and a tradition grew up for the two sons of his oldest sister to spend their school holidays at The Shop because their father and mother were in service in the south, and needed to work together. They loved to come and help, especially with killing rabbits!

CWJ always felt responsible for his family, because he was the oldest boy, and there were strong ties of affection. He was always

Cusins Peter and Cyril with the sheep at Rorrington

slightly puzzled that EMJ did not feel the same about her family. In fact she was, and always had been, the family peacemaker. As a child, she had to sit next to her father at meals because the others argued and he slapped them. Later, she was often the only one on speaking terms with all her family at once. On the whole, in this family, I liked the aunts and uncles by marriage better than the blood relations.

EMJ loved her mother, whereas some of her sisters preferred their father whom they called by the Welsh name of Dada. She also felt a strong sense of duty and affection towards her oldest sister, Lizzie, who took on a lot of family responsibilities, including looking after the mentally handicapped sister. Lizzie ran the family home for many years, and looked after the three illegitimate sons born in the family. EMJ helped by having them to visit and stay, but was not willing to 'adopt' one of them, or another sister's child, although it was suggested she should when it appeared that she would be married but childless. Her brother, who was also childless, was persuaded to give a home, and later, work, to one of the illegitimate group, and it was never a happy relationship.

Both EMJ and CWJ were comfortable with the way the other would work away at something and see it through to the end. He had always wanted to do well, but now he found his ambitions expanding. He wanted to give her what she had lost — the status and the income that went with a real farm and, for her family, the education and training which had been whisked from her grasp. While he had started out in life as a poor boy and she came from the slightly higher class of tenant farmers, the slump in farming after the war changed their positions. Her family, with a bankrupt father, one brother dead and one soon to start on his own account, and a smallholding in the name of the oldest sister, became poorer than his which had the earning power or potential of several men. It is interesting to notice the occupations the young people from CWJ's and EMJ's families chose: her family were moving into nursing and teaching, in his family the girls went into service and some of the boys worked on farms. He had to do well, therefore, not just by working-class standards, but by middle-class ones. Within ten years of their marriage, and maybe from the start, he was thinking in terms of partnership, of 'we' rather than 'I', and within that ten years he had achieved much. Often you feel he would have said to himself, 'I must work harder'. EMJ worked hard too and was the calm centre of his universe.

In her turn, she could hardly believe that anything so wonderful could happen to her. She adored him. He was tall and good-looking. She often stressed how, in the early days, if you looked at a crowd, he would stand out as the tallest. He had a motor-bike, so he could take her about, even faster than Kitty, her father's pony, who used to be the fastest thing on the roads around Chirbury. He was ambitious, go-ahead and prepared to take risks as well as work hard; and he loved her with devotion. She knew that she could sew well enough to keep herself looking smart, and her cooking was better than any he had been used to. She was fortunate that the First World War ended when it did.

Two older men, Mr Evans of Wotherton Hall and Mr Hughes of Marton Hall, helped CWJ with know-how and practical advice when he was starting to farm. He also had a friend of about his own age, John Owen of Llewynrhedydd, who, with his wife Maggie, struggled with their own small farm, and later moved to Cwm Duggan on the Long Mountain.

However, the nearest and most important neighbours at Rorrington were 'Farmers the Green', consisting of Mr and Mrs Farmer and their son Jack. They lived about quarter of a mile away down a steep lane. All three spoke broad dialect. She was a large stout woman, known for being a Mrs Malaprop. When she first saw a bungalow, she came home with a tale of a 'bungle hole'. She spoke of seeing someone 'in her Isabels'. I didn't get this joke so it had to be explained to me that she meant 'in her deshabille', which I still didn't know. The word must have been in more common use in the 1930s than it is now. Mrs Farmer said to CWJ, as the tiny Austin 7's brakes squealed, 'You want a drop of oil on your brakes, Cuth' and, as the little car laboured up the hill with her overflowing the passenger seat and he struggled to change gear, 'Dunna you worry about me, Cuth, I'm all right.'

Later Jack Farmer was good pals with Uncle Tom. In the morning, Jack would say 'Bist e going to Pool today, Tum?', meaning, 'if so can I have a lift?' Uncle Tom was, but he said he didn't know. 'If I am, I'll hang out the bag so you can see.' (A regular sign between the two houses in pre-telephone days). Back at home, Uncle Tom would tell my cousins not to put the bag out yet. 'Let the Bugger have time to change into his working clothes', (he would say 'beggar' not 'bugger' if my aunt or my girl cousin was there). Once the bag was hung up he would have to change again — it was still a good joke to play in return for the free lift to Welshpool.

CWJ was elected to Chirbury Parish Council, and he also took part in village concerts. He couldn't sing in tune at all, but acted in sketches, and did 'humorous recitations' which were fashionable then.

Farmers were like little kings in their own territories at that time, responsible for the money, for the well-being of the family, their workers and their animals. They looked after the comings and goings of poorer neighbours and were, (and still are) rewarded with a title such as 'Mr Morris the White House', or 'Mr Evans of Walton'. Many of them were struggling along with cheap family labour and had no time to look at new methods. CWJ had to keep ahead of the times, he had no sons for cheap labour, but he was more sophisticated, and travelled more than many of his peers.

CWJ had worked on a farm, and every boy in this country district knew about farming. But his serious training had been as a cobbler and boot-maker, and fattening and selling a few pigs was no training for being a farmer. Under the circumstances, he was lucky to get the tenancy of Rorrington Shop, where a mixture of abilities (including cobbling and cutting hair) would come together with farming to make a living in what was still a difficult time for everyone. He was, however, clear that 'proper' farming meant dealing with horses and cows, and perhaps sheep, if you had a large flock. Growing and harvesting hay and corn crops was the other sort of 'proper' farming. Pigs, poultry, the dairy and selling rabbits were all marginal, although he was happy to do it if there was money to be made.

When they married and moved to Rorrington, the farm was too small to need much labour, and what was needed could be supplied by family and friends. But his best help was even nearer home. EMJ realised that he was working so long and so hard outside that she wouldn't see him unless she did something about it. She wanted to be with him, 'so I had to work outside too, even though I hadn't been used to it'. (At Stockton, there had been plenty of cooking, cleaning and dairy work to do indoors.) So she went to work outside. They did almost everything together after this. The exception was that machinery was 'his'; to the end of her days she preferred a needle and thimble to a sewing-machine, a knife and a chopping-board to a food-processor, and she never learnt to drive.

CWJ's younger half-brothers both worked for him at different times, Dennis doing so on and off for many years. He was unfortunate in having a bad motor-cycle accident in 1933 which prevented him from working for a couple of years, and still troubled him in his 50s. He was very versatile, and could do many of the 'extras' which CWJ undertook to keep farm and shop afloat, such as cobbling and wood-working. Dennis played a big part in the success of Rorrington, and surely must have lived in for much of the time, 'home' at Wotherton being so crowded. He kept his motor-bike at Rorrington, and used it to round up the cows and sheep on the hill. Don, the sheep-dog, learnt to ride pillion.

Walter, the other half-brother, worked for CWJ for a short time 'helping, etc,' on the shop rounds in the early '30s when CWJ was a young chap driving a pony and rather muddy trap. Then he would quite often get a new job in May, when farmers would be hiring extra labour for the summer, and eventually he landed a job at Lower Stockton.

In the last couple of years at Rorrington, a new name appears in the diaries — Tom Bishop, one of a large family. He worked occasional days, usually with someone else, catching rabbits. He was to marry CWJ's sister Amy, and when CWJ finally signed the new tenancy agreement for Aldon, it was Tom and Amy Bishop who took over the holding at Rorrington, although they very sensibly realised that the village shop had had its day, and didn't take that on. Their three children grew up there, they were all around my age.

When he could, CMJ bought machines that would aid the work, like the second-hand engine which powered the milking machine. Then there was the second-hand car that gave poor Dolly the pony a break and made things easier for him.

The background noise in the memories of my childhood (albeit at the subsequent farm at Aldon) is of two soft voices talking and talking. A little blurred because I'm not listening, hushed laughter, and more talk. They were like two halves of one whole. When he was working outside and I was indoors, he would come in every now and then. 'Where's Mum?' With the super-telepathy which works between some mothers and daughters, I would tell him 'She's upstairs,' or 'In the garden' or 'Round the hens'. And off he would go to find her, as though he couldn't bear to be away from her any longer.

CWJ and EMJ thought abut farming all the time. They didn't just read a few pages in *The Farmer's Weekly*, or watch the one farming programme which used to be on television after Sunday dinner. On the road in outward journeys it would be 'Look at their corn', or 'roots' or whatever, and 'they're not so forward as us' or 'doing better than us'. On the way back it would be 'They've had a drop of rain here. Wonder what it's been like at home.'

CWJ's type of mixed farming dealt with many kinds of animals, all requiring different skills: horses, both for the land and for transport, cattle kept for the dairy and sold on for beef, sheep and pigs; and there were vermin to be killed. Hens and other poultry were of course on 'Man's side', and so were the dogs, rabbits and vermin were not, and the cats seemed to wait to decide who would win before deciding which side to join.

Horses were most important at first, both for pulling the trap in which CWJ would make the shop rounds, and for working the land. Dolly was the pony who pulled the trap, up and down those steep roads, day after day, and regularly visiting Minsterley to bring back 7½ cwt or so of coal for the round. Fortunately most people were able to save money by burning a lot of wood, so Dolly only had to bring a limited amount back up the hill to Rorrington. In her later life her work was made less by the use of a car and then van. She died in February 1938. The diary entries read:

> Saturday 26 Poor old mare dead (Doll). Had hay from
>   G Davies (Weston Bank).
> Sunday 27 Buried Doll.

She was obviously an honoured member of the team, because she was buried, not sent to the knacker, like the pony Kit, which died about the same time.

The other horse in those early days was Stanley, who was kept for farm-work. When CWJ and EMJ moved to Aldon in 1939, he stayed temporarily with the new tenants, and didn't come to Aldon till 1940. Then, because he was a good strong worker, he was sold for one guinea (£1 1s) in June that year; it was the age of the tractor, but it was wartime and fuel for tractors was not always easily obtained.

Animals were named not to make pets of them but to remember them — it's easier to remember that Buttercup had a difficult calving than to try to think whether it was number 127, 125 or 129. CWJ

Cousins Cyril and Peter with the cows at Rorrington

always preferred the cows to be out overnight if possible, and build up nice thick winter coats, but on the high ground they sometimes had to stay in overnight in the winter — that meant more clearing out and more muck-spreading, hard work with a shovel and a dray. The cows tended to have pet names, which usually either indicated their appearance or where they had been bought, (Bromlow from a nearby hamlet, or Lymore from an auction at Lymore just outside Montgomery). Some names survived in the herd for many years. Those first ones were Strawberry, Sue, Molly, Bluebell, Stapeley and Lymore, and they were joined over the next few years by Nancy, Sybil, and Roan; then there were Floss, Darkie, and Black Bess, and many others over the years, the old girls being culled and the young heifers coming into production. Pullet was a cow who got her name as a joke: EMJ could only remember the name that was given to a young hen, not a young cow, and Young Pullet was one of her calves. At first there were blue-and-white and red-and-white Ayrshire types, and some Herefords with deep red coats. The first Friesian cow was Moveage who arrived at Rorrington in 1936 from Moveage near Shrewsbury. Noddy and Gwernychair joined the herd during the war. Of course those were the dairy cows. Cattle which were sold on as fat or store animals were not recorded by name, though no doubt CWJ had his own way of remembering exactly which was which. CWJ was well in advance of many in England in mechanising the milking parlour, and an engine was installed at Rorrington in 1938. It was a dual-purpose machine that also powered the clippers used for sheep-shearing. Mechanised milking was quite rare until the 1940s and it was into the '50s before the majority of farmers had installed the machines.

Pigs at Rorrington

The milking machine arrived at Aldon in 1939; having had one at Rorrington CWJ wasn't going back to milking by hand.

Pigs were an important part of the operation in the first years at Rorrington. In 1931 the sows Betty, Rose and Tiny produced no fewer than 77 piglets between them!

Poor Betty died after her second farrowing and the following year was replaced by Silver. Swine fever hit the country in 1933. For pig farmers this can be as serious as an outbreak of foot-and-mouth disease is for all landowners, but the outbreak seems to have been short-lived since in August two pigs were sold for £2 10s and soon after a further seven went off to market.

Over the years the number of sows was increased, producing eight litters in 1935 and 14 in 1936. Piglets were mostly sold on as stores to other farmers. A few were retained and fattened and taken to Shrewsbury Smithfield, or sometimes to Welshpool, except for the one or two which would be kept for the family's use. The Movement Book records the occasional move of a pig to Victoria House (EMJ's father's home at Worthen where her sister Lizzie had the tenancy of the smallholding). CWJ would also go over there periodically to kill a pig for the family. After 1936 the pig-keeping side of the business was wound down as the dairy improved. The milk contract signed the previous year ensured a regular monthly cheque and from then on the significant buying and selling is among the cattle. When the move to Aldon happened at the end of March 1939 the move involved 113 sheep, 60 lambs, 20 cows, and 1 bull, but no sows or piglets.

Thinking about farming methods, costs and plans, was something CWJ and EMJ did naturally together, talking constantly about the issues. In the Rorrington years the aim was to get ahead by any possible means. A car or a van for the rounds, a milk contract to make use of the grass, the main hillside crop, and a bigger farm were the main objectives. By the end of ten years, all seemed well on course. Prices were still dreadfully low, and with no reserve of accumulated capital there was little chance even to buy well. The horse, Stanley, and Dolly, the pony who pulled the trap for deliveries, were still in daily use but after 1933 there was the little car and then the van to do some of the journeys; but CWJ really enjoyed working with the horses.

The more he thought about it, the more CWJ wanted to move ahead. Not just a tiny hill farm, but a proper one. Men working for him. Arable crops and tractors, not just cart-horses. A comfortable house. The Shop was comfortable enough, but not very smart, and he loved to be hospitable. The first thing to do was to get established, save every possible penny, get some better buildings and start selling milk, and all the while think about more land. He set himself a decade

CMJ feeding the sheep

to achieve something. He was already 29 when he married. He was happy enough at Rorrington, although he worked so hard he was tired.

CWJ got the estate going on building and plumbing work for the cows, dairy and pigs, and undertook to pay some cash in advance and some extra rent. The world could see that they were doing well, and were prepared to put money back into the business.

In just under a decade, 1930–1939, CWJ established a routine with the farming at Rorrington. The shop's deliveries and other business had to be done every day, but EMJ did a lot too. It was their aim to increase the numbers of sheep and cows, and to sell milk to the creamery at Minsterley from an improved herd. Progress to these ends was well on the way. The herd started with seven cows and there were sheep and pigs.

The routine was something like this: January to March bad weather; kill a pig (sometimes CWJ would go to kill a pig for his brother Dennis, or for a neighbour); do odd jobs such as building or repairing hen houses; check the horses' shoes for some mobility on bad roads — there were special nails for the icy roads. In spring there could still be some snow and cold weather, but the lambs would start to arrive.

In April and May there would be two or three days of working in the garden, and some time in June the sheep would be shorn and the hay harvest would be started; there was cutting, turning, carting, building ricks and thatching to do all at once.

The beginning of the hay harvest was actually in the spring when the cows were turned off the fields to be cut; perhaps in April there would be a note in the diary:

| 15 April 1933 | Turned off bottom meadows. |
| 18 April 1933 | Turned off stackyard meadows. |

On 14 June that year he started to harvest the meadows. At Rorrington, CWJ's family was able to help with the hay harvest, and

Harvest-time at Rorrington with cousins Peter, Margaret and Cyril

it was also a way for CWJ to help his mother with a bit of cash. Haymaking was something of a party-time for the family; Renee and Fred were sure to be there with their sons for some of the time, and Ag, and Amy and her daughter Margaret. All help was welcome, including EMJ's nephews.

A good hay harvest was fundamental to the running of the farm, and its date varied year by year. On Wednesday 24 July 1935 CWJ wrote in his diary of a harvest at Rorrington, noting how many cartloads had come from each field. In 1939, the first summer at Aldon, the harvest was later, on 26 August.

In the summer the sheep also had to be dipped twice. July and August were the months for visitors, who could sometimes help with the work.

As the farm could grow no corn there was only bought straw, so bracken was cut to use as litter for the stock when they came inside for the winter. September was the month for cutting and stacking bracken on the hill. By December there might be a dozen stacks. The ewes would go to the ram in September/October, and in November and December some cider would be made, and depending on what had happened early in the year, sometimes there would be a pig to be killed. Before Christmas there would be a spell of killing, plucking and drawing poultry for the Christmas market, and then quiet Christmas meals as the guests of family and with family guests.

All the year round there were the routine jobs of milking, looking after pigs, seeing to the mating and calving of cows, taking animals to auction and buying others. Welshpool market was on Monday, (including on Bank Holiday Monday because the local auction was so much more important than the national holiday). Other fairs were at Montgomery, Lymore and Llanfair Caereinion.

It was essential to be able to delegate work, trust that it was being done properly, and get on with the many other equally important jobs which were waiting. At, or about, the same time there were often two major tasks (for example, shearing and starting the hay harvest some weeks after moving the stock off the meadows to be cut). With hens, you had to buy in or hatch chicks, move them to the adult home, feed and water them, collect the eggs and sell them, in the end see about culling the hens, and finally kill them, dress and sell the carcases.

A small loan from the family in the early years had enabled CWJ and EMJ to get started. It was a flexible arrangement for up to 20 years and was on terms far more suited to their characters than most bank loans. There was no business plan, which meant it was easier for them to adapt to varying circumstances. And there was no requirement for the money to be used as planned when the plans had been forced to change; it was a very flexible form of borrowing.

I don't think CWJ and EMJ understood much about the principles of finance, about the percentage of profit and proportion of turnover to capital which a farm should aim for. Neither did CWJ have that other rule of thumb 'Well, it's what my father used to do ...'. EMJ had more of that, but after her father's bankruptcy she always doubted his methods. When I read now about the agricultural depression of the 1870s and 1880s, and the slow recovery, helped in the end by the First World War, only for the whole thing to crash back into depression again, I am amazed at the sophistication of the financial methods of some farmers. What a good thing CWJ didn't know or he might never have started.

He was completely innocent of all notion of tax. Insurance, yes; life assurance, yes, since they needed some provision for old age; profit, yes; but tax, no. It was better to buy something outright than rent or hire it. And, as well as earning money, you had to be as thrifty as you could.

Cottage people in those days didn't pay income tax, as they only had tiny incomes. There were no schemes then to help new businesses and explain all the regulations. But hard work, luck, a larger farm and more positive government policies during and after the Second World War brought more prosperity. One day years later there was a letter from the Inland Revenue. This was followed by many meetings, lots of paperwork and long sessions with the accountant (one of only two or three people I actually knew CWJ to dislike). I heard one discussion with EMJ that ended 'No, you must stay with the same firm [of accountants]. If you move, it can cause even more trouble and suspicion.'

I can remember CWJ sitting at the kitchen table struggling with old bills and receipts. He was not one to throw things away. Old bills were filed on rusty old spikes, chequebook stubs were kept, and of course banks can supply old records. Eventually a submission was made to the tax people, and they agreed to settle for between £4,000 and £5,000. 'Not fair' said EMJ. 'They have done it all on today's prices, forgetting how much things have changed since we started.' I never really understood the arguments, but I do know they felt seriously aggrieved, and after that set out to 'do' the tax out of every possible halfpenny. Any private cash sale which didn't have to go through the books was welcome, because there was no tax to pay. I've never spoken of this because I was warned not to, but now the records have all been thrown away and I haven't long to live! Sorry, taxman.

As for the actual farm at Rorrington, there were some obvious steps to take. The cow-houses and dairy needed to be improved, with water laid on; a milking machine obtained and eventually signed a contract with the Minsterley creamery and the milk collected — there just wasn't time to deliver it. That contract was very important, for it meant being part of the Milk Marketing Board and whilst it involved surrendering a small measure of independence, in return there came stable prices and a regular monthly milk cheque.

But CWJ was still looking forward and looking for a new and bigger farm. Although he had made improvements at Rorrington, he didn't hold back when the opportunity to move arose; they went to look at a farm at Aldon in September 1938 and took advice from a neighbour about the possible new tenancy. (It wasn't just an important week for them: that week the Munich Agreement was signed, an event that only managed the briefest mention in the diary, between

The Brooches in the 1906s — the hosue was empty

41

digging up the potatoes and picking apples.) Later, he bought extra land, first at Eaton-under-Heywood, and then a 98-acre farm called The Brooches, near Craven Arms.

CHAPTER FOUR

Aldon

Finding the new tenancy had taken quite a time. They had been looking for about five years, but they moved from 13.9 acres with some hill grazing, some extra ground and the village shop, to a proper farm of about 200 acres. Although it was still on a hillside, it was not so high and not so bleak. The farmhouse was huge for two people, and my mother said that at first her legs ached from just walking about indoors. But they were young and strong and forward-looking, with nearly ten years' experience behind them. The tenancy was signed in January 1939 and on Saturday 25 February CWJ wrote in his diary 'Ploughed first furrow on the new farm'; the entry about signing up to buy the farm's first tractor, an International, was on the same day.

The main part of the move, in March 1939, was done by rail, with wagons to move the goods from Rorrington to Forden Station and from Craven Arms to Aldon. Even with Dennis and Tom Bishop to help, the move was hard work. One of my cousins was at school in Chirbury, and she says the children were most impressed by the amount of stuff to be moved. A lot of it was probably rubbish — we have always been very good at hoarding junk.

When CWJ and EMJ moved to Aldon, they left their families 20 miles away — a huge move for them, although people were accustomed to daughters travelling long distances to go into service. Visits then were only possible because they had a car, and could still drive over to visit once a week or so. Other family members were getting cars and motor-bikes too, and there were reasonable trains and buses near Aldon, although the long valley between Shrewsbury and Montgomery was always difficult by public transport.

CWJ and EMJ arrived on the Stokesay estate to a hamlet of two farms (their own and Mr Bradley's); a smallholding (Mr Morris with a young family) and four cottages, one at least tied to each farm. But in my early childhood, between 1946 and 1953, there were 15 or so children living there, and more in outlying cottages, as every house, no matter how steep and difficult to access, was full in house-hungry post-war Britain.

Other neighbours were Mr & Mrs Pugh, living two to three fields away with seven children; Tom Jacks, Mrs Jacks and Phyllis, living at Withersley in Aldon Gutter; Mr Marsh of Stoke, living on a farm at Stokesay; and lots of families in cottages off the road. A big upheaval in population in the next few years left CWJ & EMJ as some of the longest-serving inhabitants of Aldon.

The only 'crop' at Rorrington had been grass, but Aldon was full of new opportunities. From the start at Aldon things were going to be different, there was room to grow wheat, barley and oats, and conditions were suitable with those (relatively) big fields sloping to the south-south-east. CWJ favoured oats and wheat, being less keen to grow barley. However during the war years barley had to be part of

Aldon

44

the cropping pattern, and from then on he continued to have a crop every year.

The need to provide winter fodder for the larger number of milking cows and for the sheep meant root crops had to be grown, but grass was still the most important crop. It carried sheep and cattle through much of the year, as grass throughout the summer and hay (and later, silage) through the winter. The winter-feed would be complemented with beet-pulp, mangolds, and a kibbled mixture of corn and some supplements.

Even in the 1950s it was difficult to find out much about new crops. Of course, farmers went ahead with new implements because they could find out about them from the reps. But where did you find out about silage? CWJ had been interested for some time in what little he knew of this new method of preserving grass. Possibly, if he'd been active in the NFU, he might have found something out, or if he'd been in touch (but how?) with one of the agricultural colleges. He would have benefited from a professional development programme from a nearby college or university — except that we didn't call farming a profession then. As it was, one day, when CWJ was driving us home from Worcester he stopped and said 'That's the place'. We had stopped at a farm and he went into the stackyard. EMJ told me he was trying to find out as much as he could about silage. As a result railway sleepers became the next thing CWJ needed to get, and pretty soon there was a silage clamp in the stackyard at Aldon.

Labour was so hard to get that first year on the larger farm that CWJ was driven back to his own family. Thus, in the first months at Aldon, there were plenty of visits from the family, especially as Tom and Amy had taken over the tenancy of The Shop and were bringing some stuff over gradually. One of the last to move was the carthorse, Stanley. Once it became clear that the War was real, CWJ tried to get hold of as much petrol as possible to have in reserve — he knew how important the family was to him. He, who hated paperwork, was also prepared to fill in forms later to try to get extra petrol for visiting sick and elderly relations where public transport was impossible.

In the early days at Aldon one of the tied cottages was let to some people called Hughes, who presumably wanted to be in a safe zone (these were the early days of the War). Tied cottages were relatively new to CWJ and EMJ, who still expected to find it easy to get local labour rather than use the cottages for their workers. But even if letting the cottage brought in a little extra cash, it was a bad move, as the Hugheses let large rent arrears pile up. When it came to the National Farm Survey, it was clear that shortage of labour was a problem, and the lack of accommodation only made matters worse.

In the summer of the year I was born, 1943, Bill Gittoes started work as a live-in youth at 17 shillings a week. His passion was the cinema, and he used to walk to Craven Arms three evenings a week to see the films; there was a different programme for Monday to Wednesday, for Thursday to Saturday, and on Sunday. It was not long before Bill suggested that his father, Harry, might be available too — and that is why I still write 'Bill and Harry',

Amy who, with her husband Tom took ove the tenancy of The Shop

with Bill first although he was the son, and always called 'William' by his dad. The whole family was short, as though they had not had enough to eat in childhood. As he got older, Bill got rather fat.

Harry and his wife moved into one of the tied cottages, and packed themselves into it with two sons, Jim and Harry (Jim was still at school) and two daughters, just about the age to be going away to work. When Jim left school he came to work on the farm in the old-fashioned way, but fairly soon left. He tried to get into the Royal Navy but failed the selection test. He was not a very good character, and the police found out once or twice that he had broken in to the house and stolen a few items. He never admitted it, and there was never a list of

46

what was missing, so for many years every time an item was lost, it was a case of 'Perhaps Jim had it'.

During the Second World War farmers had to make use of whatever labour they could find. At the end of September 1940 CWJ recorded the help of some 'college boys' who were cutting wood at Aldon. They were at the farm for a week again during the spring sowing season the following year. These were almost certainly boys from Lancing College who had been evacuated from Sussex to Stokesay Court, and their stay there also gave CWJ an extra outlet for farm produce: he occasionally supplied eggs, rabbits and poultry. They were not the only strangers to work on the farm during the war. 1943 brought some Italian prisoners of war to Aldon: two of them arrived in May when CWJ was trying to get the sugar beet hoeing finished and the weather was impeding the task. A note in the diary tells us they were useful workers: '2 POWar — very good'. We don't know how long those two were at the farm, but when the hay harvest started CWJ made an enquiry about POW labour and two men came again and worked for about a week. There was also quite a lot of sharing of labour, apparently according to which farmer was doing what and where help was needed, so there are regular mentions of, for example, 'Bill, Jarrett's, half-day' or 'Threshing barley. Tom only from Mr Norris 5 hrs'; 'Phillis at Mr Norris potatoes'. It was all part of how country people adapted their lives and their working ways to the reality of the war.

Several other young chaps from round about got a few months' or years' experience working on the farm, but Bill and Harry stayed on and there was never any question about their honesty or time-keeping, although they did love to talk. Somewhere I have a photo of Bill and Harry, one on either side of the vet's car, holding on and talking, as he tried to drive away. When Bill married he moved into the cottage next door to his parents which had conveniently become vacant around that time since Derek Pinches, who had been working at Aldon, had moved on. Eventually Harry retired, and CWJ retired after helping Bill to find another job. He and his family (he was married and had two daughters) moved to Craven Arms after living in Aldon for some 25 years.

At the time CWJ and EMJ moved to Aldon, Squire Allcroft of the Stokesay estate seemed to be trying to modernise. In their first summer in their new home at Aldon there was much talk of possible war and evacuation. All this made them the more keen to get on with the alterations which the estate had promised — a new cow-house, refurbishing of the dairy and a bathroom and inside lavatory.

Markets in Ludlow and Craven Arms were relatively near, but Shrewsbury remained about 20 miles away, and Welshpool was further than before. Oswestry was too far, but Bridgnorth now came into the picture. Once again a car was a lifeline for all around.

This was farming as they had not known it. There were big fields, needing strong skilled labour as well as the newly-bought second-hand

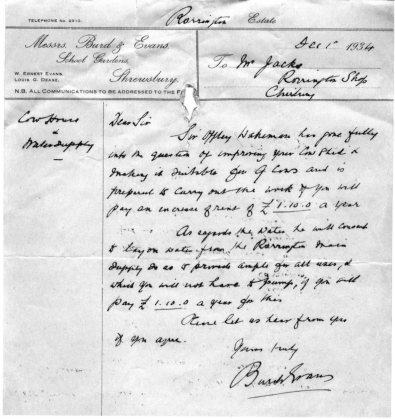

The letter from the Rorrington Estate in December 1934 agreeing to carry out work to the cow-house and laying on a water main for the additional annual rent of £1 10 shillings for each item

tractor, the horses and the milking-machine engine. Rabbits waged constant war, but their bodies could be sold. There was still a pig kept for the house, eggs to sell, and family to visit. This now usually meant picking them up, and having them to stay overnight. Even when they were not fully two months in the house they were giving Amy, CWJ's youngest sister, and her new husband, Tom, hospitality for their honeymoon. CWJ tried to organise help in the house as well as on the farm, but it fell through. But EMJ was probably pleased — provided she could keep up with the work she preferred to be alone, working at her own pace.

It was 1946 before there was a baler at Aldon to make a bit lighter the work of gathering in the hay, and the first corn harvest using a combine appears to have been in 1953 — it was a very expensive piece of machinery and like the old threshing machine it went from farm to farm.

One of the forward moves on the farm was to the accreditation of the herd as tuberculin-tested: it meant selling the cows who failed or were doubtful when the test results came back; they went to the market at Shrewsbury. CWJ always used to listen with keen interest to the market prices on Wednesday mornings, to hear the price of his own and others' stock. 'How do you *know*?' I asked. 'Well, they don't say 'CW Jacks of Aldon got so much. But if they mention £126 10s, and that's what I got, then at least I know we were equal first.' At around that time he had a nice suit made at Ronald Back's, with a thread of nice dark greenish-blue woven in the fine tweed. It cost a bit less than a cow. Certainly the rest of the outfit, shirt, tie, socks and shoes, would have taken it up to or beyond the cow's price.

Cream would be skimmed by hand from the top of the milk, not actually reducing the butterfat content very much. Every 10 to 14 days the enamel bucket would be full, representing the cream from 100 to 150 churns. The bucket of cream was warmed gently using the precious and irreplaceable pre-war German butter thermometer (which I wasn't allowed to touch) to tell when the right temperature was reached. The cream then went into the spotlessly clean churn and the lid was clamped shut. We then turned the handle steadily until the cream 'came'. There was a window in the churn so you could see if the liquid inside was starting to run clear instead of sticking to the glass. You would also hear a thud as you churned if a lump of butter was forming. The buttermilk might be given to pigs or cats and dogs.

EMJ would take the butter to the earthenware sink and wash it in running water, salt it, and 'work' it to get rid of any remaining buttermilk. She would then divide it up accurately into half-pounds, using a pretty wooden pat with ridged edges and a design of a swan. She made oblong half-pounds with ridged tops, wrapped them in greaseproof paper and cooled them, so that they set as much as possible. I used to plead for some round pats with the pretty swan design, and there were usually a few. The butter was always softer and saltier than today's commercial butter.

During the war the emphasis was on milk and crops. For a few years CWJ bought young pigs to fatten — at Aldon he had the space to rear them, and we killed a pig at home until the mid-'50s, but the focus after the war was on the dairy herd and sheep. I remember him once saying 'There are some *new* piglets. Do you want to come and see them?' The sow was still drowsy and contented, letting them suckle as they wanted. Later it would be a fierce battle. I wanted to stroke one — they looked so delicately pink with silky white hair. I don't remember how CWJ persuaded the mother to let me handle one of her new piglets, but he did, and I was so disappointed. It was bristly, not silky at all! Swine fever struck again in 1953, this time at our neighbours, the Jarretts' farm, and CWJ had to destroy a litter of 11 piglets that February. It probably wasn't as a result of the disease, but pigs were not seen again at Aldon Farm after 1954.

Rearing pigs always meant killing them. I'd know what was to take place and I'd be in a panic because I *hated* the blood and the terror and the squealing. At first EMJ would take me out in the fields somewhere and not bring me back till it was all over. Then there was a short time when CWJ was able to borrow the humane killer from the abattoir in Craven Arms over lunch-time and use it to stun the pig before cutting its throat. It was explained to me that the pig must be empty of blood or its meat would be all wrong. Sometimes CWJ helped others with their pigs, for it wasn't a job one man could do alone.

EMJ and I would return to find that Bill and Harry had helped CWJ drive the pig into the backyard where they had killed it, and they would be scalding and scraping the skin. They would remove the trotters, then hang the carcass from a huge beam in the back kitchen, slice it open and remove its guts and put them in a big bath. Some parts would be wanted: the liver and the intestines. I don't think we used the lights but every bit of fat was saved for scratchins and, most importantly, lard.

The carcase was then left to cool, and when it was firm and set it would be divided up into flitches to be salted for bacon, hams to be salted, and some fresh meat. I never liked pork, so I wasn't interested in this part, but I liked to watch the bacon and ham being salted. The meat was rubbed with saltpetre and salt, and turned and rubbed again and again, until eventually it was hung up to dry. 'We don't like our bacon smoked, so we don't hang it in the smoke, but they do in some parts of the country,' I was told.

Meat for sausages and pork pies had been put aside all the time, cut up into cubes and put in a large bowl, and any meat which would yield lard and scratchins was simmered until they could be separated. Scratchins were a treat for a few mouthfuls, then quickly became too rich. CWJ would manage some more for bait.

Meanwhile, EMJ would have unpacked and scalded the mincer, and when, perhaps by the next evening, she had managed to wash and scrape the intestines for sausage skins (a truly horrible job) we would have a few trial runs through the mincer with bread cubes and meat and sage. It would go through the mincer again with meat, so it didn't matter what shape or colour it was at this first stage. Then the work started in earnest, gruelling hard work. A long skin was fed over the tube leading out of the mincer, and handfuls of meat, bread and sage fed in. We took it in turns to turn the handle whilst someone — EMJ was best at it — had to measure off the sausages and tie them up in those attractive links you used to see in good butchers' shops. That evening we might have a supper of sausages, to eat up all the odd-shaped ones, and the ones which were nearly all bread when you were cleaning the mincer at the end. Mmm! I don't know that anything ever tasted so good. And after working for a few hours in the back kitchen, even with a paraffin stove, it was lovely to come back into the warm kitchen to cook and eat.

EMJ would also make pies and brawn over the next few days, often whilst I was at school. Parcels would be made up of various pies and products to post or take to those who were on that time's list, or those with whom you swapped fresh produce when you each killed a pig.

51

CWJ had started in sheep before the war, his first flock being a funny-looking mixed lot with ewes with a variety of black or white or mottled faces. Some were Cluns, some were Kerries, and some were cross-bred. Then, because there was grazing on the hill that came with the farm tenancy, CWJ went to Llanfair sheep auction and bought some Welsh sheep. In their new home the Welsh sheep just had to manage as best they could on the hill, and CWJ's diary shows that every few days he went 'round Welsh'.

In 1931, at Rorrington, 18 ewes were shorn; between them they had had 15 lambs. This looks poor beside today when an average of two lambs per ewe from a pure breed would be expected. In 1931 it was not even one lamb per ewe; by my childhood in the 1950s, you expected a lamb and a half.

During the war the flock, in line with national policy, decreased sharply. By the time I first remember, it was starting to increase again, and even a cade (orphan) lamb was precious, although every effort was made to foster them. The first cade lamb I remember was Ann who was fortunately female and so joined the relatively long-lived breeding stock of those days.

The sheep didn't have pretty names like the cows and some of the sows, but were referred to as the 'sandy-faced ewe', 'Tan-faced 3-year-old ewe', 'Blacknose' or 'Nip-eared theave' (I follow CWJ's spelling) and 'Little Twin'. One ewe seems to have been named for her character rather than her looks, she was called 'Boss'! And there was an old lady called

Me bottle-feeding Ann, the first orphan lamb I can recall

'Granny' who got things off to a good start by having three lambs in 1931. But the risk of death is closer with older animals, and she died soon afterwards. Presumably it was her daughter who was called 'Young Granny'.

What a nuisance it must have been to have someone (student-age me) with the time and perfectly willing to help when asked, but not actually taking responsibility for any jobs. Yes, I have walked round the ewes and lambs, and carried two wet, heavy, newly-born lambs up a field in an icy

Still undertaking the bottle-feeding when a few years older

wind for half a mile, with the ewe sullenly charging me all the time. 'It'll be better when we get you out of the wind, old lady' is impossible to say. EMJ did the late shift, CWJ the early shift, so with my night-owl tendencies, I used to see more of her. The NFU in Craven Arms ran a 'Lamb Bank' — that is, anyone who had an extra lamb or two suitable for fostering rang in, and so did we if we wanted one. Then you were put in touch, got the directions, and went to collect the lamb. I enjoyed that job and saw some amazing places — farms tucked away down tiny lanes in the beautiful hills, and Clun, for example. I wasn't very happy about negotiating the price — a lamb might cost between 17s and 22s 6d, quite a substantial sum of money.

I think CWJ liked his sheep, because for most of the year he would manage them on his own with a dog or two, or he could easily take EMJ to see them. But I was startled, late in the 1950s, to hear of Ann again. It seemed she had become a wise old leader of the all-female flock, and the others followed her. Ann had never been quite sure whether she was a human or a sheep, so when she saw CWJ at the gate, she would rush towards him, the rest of the flock following more slowly. He didn't need the dogs when he visited them to check their well-being.

53

With the chickens when aged one-and-a-half

I remember his telling me in the late '40s or early '50s that the most sheep he'd ever had was 333, including that year's lambs, which probably meant a flock of around 170 ewes.

Then there were the poultry. To start with, at Rorrington, it was a case of selling a single hen. Then they started to buy equipment (an incubator, special 'houses' for raising small chicks in the warmth) and some henhouses. Eventually, Dennis, CWJ's half-brother, built some henhouses, and a full-scale brooder-house was bought; it was an expensive investment so in 1939 it was taken down and re-assembled at Aldon. They also began to buy day-old chickens as well as raising their own.

Sales outlets were varied. A few were doubtless sold through the Shop and sometimes they would supply eggs for hatching to other farmers, as well as selling eggs for the table. Eggs had a steady sale in the '30s, although the price at market varied. Dressed chickens were sold on a large scale at Christmas, but there was a steady trade in these most of the year.

The hens used to run about the stackyard until they gradually got taken to henhouses or indoors to produce more eggs. Some of the henhouses were 'down the field' which meant a walk of a quarter of a mile or more several times a day, to let the hens out, to shut them up for the night, to take food and water, and to collect eggs. Walking down the field we used to see crows flying away from a raid on next door's walnut trees. If we were noisy, and lucky, the crows might drop us a walnut. What a treat!

One evening EMJ found the hens outside one of the henhouses and the fox in possession. She shut him in, and went for CWJ and the gun. On a similar occasion, but years later, I was unsuccessful. The hens were sitting around outside, dazed and comatose. I shut the door of the house and went for my father's gun, but returned to find no fox. Perhaps he had already fled the scene.

CWJ and EMJ tried battery cages for their hens, and I saw them when they first came. Everything a hen could want, and no access for foxes! But it soon seemed that the hens didn't like them, so they didn't last long. CWJ and EMJ often said that if an animal wasn't happy, it wouldn't do well. So the poor old hens didn't stay long in those dreadful wire cages. Parts of the barn and the old stables were therefore turned into deep litter houses. The hens had lots of straw; the litter was only rarely cleared out, so they built up a nice warm floor, rather like a compost heap. Electric lights on time-switches gave them spring and summer day-lengths at the seasons when eggs were most profitable. Creatures of habit, they loved to be fed and watered by the same person each day, so going away and leaving the hens was a serious business.

There were times when, however careful we were about checking, a determined predator would still get in. In the spring of 1951 it wasn't a fox that was making trouble but a neighbour's dog. One night eight hens were killed, another night six hens and a duck were lost — there were four attacks before EMJ rang the local police for advice, but the diary doesn't tell us what happened to the dog — it was a busy time, harvest was underway and CWJ's notes moved on to other priorities. The duck would have been one of a small number kept for local sale and sometimes to a butcher in Ludlow.

As more and more large specialist producers came on-stream to meet the demand they did have a few years without the grind of egg and chicken production.

CWJ was always closely followed by one or more dogs. They were never allowed in the house, but unless they were actually fastened up somewhere, you could tell which door he had gone in by, because they were waiting there. At Rorrington, *the* dog was Dan, who was very clever but whose main fault was running away. However he always came back. He survived the move to Aldon and lived there for a time.

Then there was Bonnie, a pretty, prim, black and white bitch. By the time I remember, she was an elderly lady, her eyes clouded with cataracts. But her offspring were Flash and Spark. Flash lived a restricted life in a kennel with Mr and Mrs Gittoe, but Spark was our working dog, black and white and a bit snappish. He would often rush out to meet CWJ driving the lorry, but one day when he turned to follow the lorry home, he forgot how long the wheel-base was and was run over by the back wheel. His eyes were bad but no-one had known.

This was dreadful. No working dog. To a man who looks after stock, and is used to trained dogs, this was a disaster. CWJ took to stopping the car and speaking to everyone he saw with a working dog. One day, where he and I were coming back from visiting EMJ in Aberdovey, where she was staying with her sister for the benefit of the sea air for her asthma, it paid off. A man said that his working bitch was due to pup soon, and CWJ could have a pup at an agreed price. They struck a bargain and in due course we went back to collect Lassie — black and white with a little bit of tan above her eyes. She grew and learned and worked and loved, and was clever with the animals. Then she had pups. I only saw two, and called them (with infant inspiration!) Spot and Rover: Rover was dim, and didn't live all that long. Spot was clever, and was our darling worker and playmate for many years.

Soon after this, Lassie disappeared. CWJ searched the countryside for her driving miles away on the report of a strange dog. In the end, he concluded the gypsies had stolen her. Poor Lassie. We could only hope that she soon went to a good home where her cleverness was valued.

In the meantime, Spot, who was really too young to learn, simply had to. She learnt the whistles and spoken commands for 'come', 'sit', 'get by', 'left' and 'right'. She learned how to round up and drive sheep and cattle using quite different skills. She learned to walk to heel, so she never needed a lead. If CWJ wasn't there, Spot would make valiant attempts to work for EMJ and even for me. I was desperate to be able to whistle properly so I could imitate the whistled commands which carry so well. Eventually I did make progress. Spot rode happily in the boot of the car, or on the back of the lorry or Land Rover. In a thunderstorm she would be terrified and cry to be shut in the boot for safety. She moved into the back yard and lived there, sharing a bed (a large box lined with an old blanket) and often food with families of cats, and often having a cat scratch her ears or her tummy.

Spot

Every now and then someone would give CWJ a dog, and someone once gave him a bitch. She was no good, but she had pups and one of these, called Fly, was a star. She was the most loyal little bitch in the world — a real one-person dog. She would hardly take food from anyone but CWJ, although later on a spell at the vet's for an injury taught her to trust and love the vet. She was a good many years younger than Spot, but they worked together. I can remember them doing something which you couldn't have taught them, they must have worked it out for themselves. I was driving the Land Rover slowly towards the farm amongst the sheep

whilst CWJ was jumping in and out of the passenger seat. Spot and Fly were trotting along behind. Suddenly there were no dogs. On we went. A little while later we came to a lane where we needed to turn to the left. If the dogs had gone home, it looked as though we'd both have to run with the sheep, to prevent them taking the wrong turning. But when we go to the lane, Spot and Fly were waiting there. They must have got through the hedge and run ahead to block the lane. They grinned to let us know they knew how clever they were.

When CWJ retired, Fly went to a good home with CWJ's youngest brother, who was also liked by dogs. But to me the saddest was the loss of Spot. She lived till I was 20 or more. I was home as a student when CWJ said to me 'Come and see poor old Spot; I've got her warm in the barn. She won't live long.' So I went to say goodbye to my dear old friend.

Pheasants were considered pests and were much hated by the tenant farmers. They might wander at will through fields and woods, eating what they chose, damaging crops, and, when they were finally shot, producing a cash crop for the estate but nothing for the farmers. Anyone who 'accidentally' came across a pheasant stunned by a blow from a passing car was delighted. The keepers would at least come round twice a year with a brace of pheasants, and there was an invitation to 'the farmers' shoot' at the end of the season. I don't know how other farmers did, but we always had plenty of pheasants — but not from the shoot, to which CWJ never went! CWJ was always interested in knowing where the keepers were going to be near, for then he wouldn't even take a gun out. 'You see, when I shoot, I don't miss. That might make them suspicious.' Sometimes there were so many pheasants in the larder that EMJ would laugh and say, 'Don't bring any more for a bit.' But he was lawless and enjoyed challenging authority. Sometimes he wouldn't need to shoot the pheasants. When he was feeding the young stock in one of the fields, he would often send one dog round the stock and one round the birds. The birds would run in panic against a wire-netting fence, where he would then pick up one or two and knock them on the heads

At Aldon young corn, roots and beans could all be devastated by rabbits — they came out of the woods overnight and would nibble their way through half or a third of a field of the newly shooting crops. It was heart-breaking. Friends and neighbours would go rabbiting, using a variety of methods: shooting, nets or ferrets. Some of my older cousins would arrive, change into old clothes, and go straight out with a gun.

Keepers and farmers watched each other warily. Farmers knew the keepers killed predators to give the pheasants an easy life, but shouldn't those predators have been giving the rabbits a hard time? CWJ knew where the keepers went in the woods, I remember he showed me their pathways and the gibbets where they hung the corpses of their victims — stoats and jays, for example. This was supposed to make other stoats and jays keep away out of fear of a similar fate, I was told.

The rabbits were a problem for years at Rorrington, but they were a problem that could be turned into cash or a hot dinner.

During the war, rabbits really came into their own as meat and this was reflected in the price of rabbits as in everything else. In the winter of 1939/1940 the price rose from 10d for a couple that August to 3s 3½d, before falling away to 1s 6d in May. Rabbits caught at Aldon could be taken either to JP Wood's in Craven Arms or to Peachey's in Ludlow; both were better than the market because they were open 5½ days a week. After the war sales of rabbits for meat declined rapidly; CWJ's last reference to taking some to sell in Ludlow was in 1949 but he didn't record the sale price. By then there had already been conversations, which continued for some years, with the landowner's agent about rabbit-proofing the fences to reduce the damage to the crops. The Stokesay estate under Mrs Rotton's rule was extremely helpful to farmers, and there was help with putting up rabbit-proof netting between woods and fields. Later I remember that the estate might supply the netting but you had to put it up yourself.

Like everyone else, we had plenty of rabbit in our diet. It was good too. Then in 1953 myxomatosis arrived (although this is not mentioned in the diaries) and CWJ started to use gas to control these pests. After that he made no more notes about shooting or netting rabbits.

The weather can be the farmers' greatest help or his biggest enemy. It's probably true to say that we only remember unusual weather — the bad winters of 1947 and 1963 or the hot summers of the mid 1970s. So, only unusually good days or bad storms got noted in CMJ's diaries, despite every farmer's obsession with the weather. As now, there were some hot and sunny days in summer, some lovely mild days in winter. But always it seemed as though 'nature' caught up with itself. If it was too dry in the summer for the grass to grow, there might be a mild green November.

Everyone listened to the forecast on the wireless, but the weather glasses were just as important. 'What's the glass say?' or 'Where's the glass?' he was often heard to say, meaning where is the needle pointing? A little tap on the top of the glass would often produce a small movement of the needle up or down. This, together with a very few bald indications on the dial (calm; set fair; change; rain; stormy) was the total information you could expect. The glass was newer than the barometer, a pretty antique from a saleroom and always one of EMJ's favourites. When we first had it, it broke and all the mercury escaped. It was wonderful stuff to play with, but dangerous. Eventually someone dumped it in the sink and away it ran down the drains. Someone took the barometer away and repaired it so that it too foretold the weather, but the conditions 'set fair' and 'change' are wrongly calibrated and mental adjustments have to be made.

I dimly remember bad weather each winter, so that we couldn't go down the lane. There would be huge icicles, and much groaning and bad temper from those who had to do the work. The worst weather I remember at Aldon was in 1947. I was 3½ and I can remember that the road was blocked with snow. The farmers, again working together, tried to get the milk down to Onibury — if the milk couldn't get out of course there'd be no milk payment. A track-laying vehicle of some kind was brought to help, but about half way down it went into the ditch. Everybody went to try to dig it out — I can remember going with EMJ, taking my seaside bucket and spade to help! In the end the milk churns were dug out, by which time the milk was frozen solid. Before her death, EMJ and I talked about 1947 wondering why we could not remember the power cuts which were so widespread that winter. The answer was easy when she remembered that we didn't have electricity at Aldon until 1952!

We expected to wake on winter mornings to find lacy frost patterns inside our bedroom windows, to know that the water-pipes in the buildings, if not in the house, were frozen and to find enormous icicles which we could break off and crunch like ice lollies. Snow was usually wet stuff which blocked the lane, but sometimes it was right for sledging and that was fun. The biggest joy of the winter weather, though, was

My attempt to help clear snow!

skating on the frozen pond. It wasn't very big, just a patch of muddy water, on which the boys skated at the deep end and the little girls had to keep to the shallow end. Bigger girls didn't skate — they were too busy indoors, and anyway it was too childish. We had no special clothes for any of this, just what we normally wore. Perhaps some of the good skaters wore special shoes but I had my usual Wellingtons. One cold winter EMJ found me a pair of trousers which one of my male cousins had left behind and I put them on underneath my skirt and coat for extra warmth.

After months of cold, dark winter, illuminated briefly by the bright lights of Christmas, it was wonderful to get round to March and April, to want to be outside again and to delight in tadpoles, primroses, bulbs, new grass and so on. We even deliberately made the last few weeks of winter harder for ourselves by giving things up for Lent. There was nothing to do with this chilly and bleak season, simply wait and look forward to its end. Then there would be warm wet days in spring, when it was too wet to work the land, and rainless days when the young crops were longing for water. It was usually hot some of the time in summer and wet in August. It was certainly always hot when I had to fetch the cows — usually in harvest time. They were keen to get home to be milked and went as quickly as they could, so all I had to do was open and shut gates and walk along the road behind them in case of any stragglers. But somehow it always seemed to be baking hot with thousands of flies.

Summer brought thunderstorms as well, with exciting thunder and lightning. We quickly learned to avoid being caught in the open and that thunder would never hurt us while lightning might. But we couldn't teach the dogs that. They always wanted to run and hide in a

As a youngster with the cows

dark place for safety. Often we would shut them in, as the kindest way to deal with their distress.

As soon as the sheep were shorn it would turn wild and windy — poor old sheep. Rain was particularly important on this high, sloping ground, where crops and the grazing were mainly higher than the thick woodland. If the rain didn't come at the right time after sowing, the drought, helped by rabbits and perhaps the much-hated pheasant, would ruin the crops.

CHAPTER FIVE
Life at Aldon

The house at Rorrington was quite small, with a chilly back kitchen, and the shop taking up one good room. None of the houses that my grandparents lived in had indoor sanitation, and there was no running hot water. You were lucky to have running cold water, rather than buckets, and of course it was everyone's first concern to get water laid on for the stock.

The house at Aldon, where I grew up, was different. For one thing, its core was really old — probably fifteenth century. It was a half-timbered long-house, with later additions. The house faced south and slightly west; the ground on which it stood sloping away also south and west, slightly more so to the west. To enter the house at the eastern end of the south face, you went up three steps; at the back a small trench had been dug out to keep damp soil away from the timber.

The eastern entrance led into the kitchen, warm in winter from the post-Austerity Rayburn (before that, there was a black-leaded range and a paraffin stove for cooking in summer). If you were 6ft tall you had to duck to go through the doors and under the big central

Playing on the steps at Aldon

beams in most rooms. We were puzzled because, while the main roof timber ran more or less east/west, the massive ceiling beam in the kitchen ran north/south, holding up the floor in the room above, with one end above a window and the other above a door. The kitchen floor was laid with good, well-fitting brick-shaped tiles, on which went a carpet by the 1950s. One large window looked south to the yard, and two smaller ones north, one into the backyard, and one into the back kitchen.

Apart from the external entrance into the kitchen, there were four more doors. One led up a narrow wooden staircase to what had been the men's sleeping quarters over the kitchen and the dairy. This room over the dairy was removed in 1940 when the dairy was upgraded by the estate. Another led into a big cupboard under the stairs, a third into the back kitchen. This was a high room — the one room that reached the full height of the house, up to the underside of the tiles which here took the place of slates. The roof timbers also ran at right-angles to the rest of the house. This room was partly dug into the rising ground, so when you stood at the sink and looked out of the window, you were about the same height as the flowers in the bed outside. There were three taps at this sink — hot, cold and soft water, which came from the soft-water tank outside. It could be used for washing if the proper supply failed, but though we often had no water, I never remember soft water being used except for watering the garden. The room held two large, strong tables, two brick hot-water boilers where you lit a fire under a copper, a churn for making butter, and a door leading into the backyard where the coal and sticks were kept. EMJ enjoyed fetching in a bit of coal at edge of night, and chopping a few sticks. The room always had ten or twelve egg-boxes holding several trays (I don't remember just how many) which each held 30 eggs. A full box was too heavy for me to lift on my own, although EMJ and I could lift one between us, and often did on alternate Fridays, when the Packing Station lorry came to collect them.

The remaining door from the kitchen led into a passageway off which a door on the south side opened into a little room which our predecessors used as an entrance, but for us was a pantry. The far end of the passageway opened into the dining room, and all the rest of the width of the house was occupied by the huge chimney and the bread-oven, then blocked up and unused. The dining-room was much the same size as the kitchen and had more elaborately-worked timbers in the ceiling. It had windows facing south and north, and doors east and west because you needed to walk right through it to the next passageway. This was probably once part of a large stone-flagged room into which the front door opened. Since then, a pantry and a small sitting-room had been partitioned off, and a further room built on the end of the house. The main polished oak staircase ran up from the hall, and another damp, uneven staircase led down to the cellar under the new sitting-room.

Upstairs, there was a corridor that ran along the south side of the house, so that three bedrooms got almost no sun at all. There was also a bathroom and, over the kitchen, what used to be the men's bedroom. Nice and warm but not in very good condition in our time, it housed the immersion heater, the loft ladder, and a lot of junk, and was used by CWJ as a changing-room.

When CWJ and EMJ first moved to Aldon, he tried to get a live-in maid-servant; after all, it was what farmers' wives used to have. One was engaged, and seems to have worked for a short time. Even after the war a few people still had full-time maids, but not many. However, EMJ liked to be on her own, and in the end was quite happy to be left with the vacuum cleaner, the washing machine that was eventually acquired and electric iron, while she sang or whistled about the housework.

Cleaning, with tiled or polished oak floors, black-leaded grates, 23 windows, and the dust from open fires, was a job for many hands. A little later Mrs Ashton, a widow who lived nearby, was glad of the money for cleaning, and we liked her so much. She would be down on her hands and knees polishing the floors. She got married again to a Mr Owen, and with the more formal manners of those days, we had to change from calling her 'Mrs Ashton' to 'Mrs Owen'. Not easy. But we soon lost her anyway; the black-leaded grates downstairs also went, and there were more carpets.

EMJ's working day was split between housework and cooking (including picking the vegetables and fruit), going round the hens carrying heavy buckets of grain and water, and perhaps round other animals if CWJ was busy with harvest, or not at home. She would garden a bit, or arrange flowers in the afternoon or on a light evening, or go out for a ride in the car or Land Rover to look at the crops or the stock. After dark she would clean eggs. When I think back to the '40s, '50s and '60s, I can't remember CWJ or EMJ sitting down in a comfortable chair without falling asleep. In fact, he would fall asleep sitting on a wooden kitchen chair at the table over tea, or reading to me when I was ill.

Everything in the house was arranged for CWJ's convenience and liking, including the food he liked and going out when he wanted. At first I misread this, and thought it was working men who had everything as they liked. Later, I became the pampered only child who had what she wanted. I thoroughly recommend it — I loved being the petted only one. 'Only children are always spoilt' clamoured my aunts. CWJ and EMJ smiled and nodded and went their own way, spending on my toys and clothes and education. Later still, I realised that once again this couple was doing as they thought right, in the face of common opinion, and doing it without a fuss.

Meals were probably old-fashioned even then. You got breakfast when you got up if you wanted — tea or coffee, toast, butter and marmalade. Bait came about 9.30, when CWJ came in from working outside; it might be bacon and eggs (and we were particularly fond of double-yolked eggs), mushrooms or tomatoes if they were in season, or it might be a boiled egg, a bit of fish, cold meat, or left-over pie, or cheese and biscuits with milky coffee or cocoa. Those who, like me in later years, had only just got up, had breakfast. Dinner at 1pm was the main meal of the day. Preparation for this started days, or even months in advance. Meat was bought once a week, and cut to size for cooking. Vegetables, herbs and most fruit came from the garden, which had been set the previous April/May; in summer and autumn you went round the most likely apple and plum trees and blackberry patches, looking for fruit.

Preparing vegetables was a chilly business in winter, but I learnt to cook by 'helping' to get dinner, chopping the vegetables, making the custard, laying and clearing the table. If pudding was to be a fruit pie, it would be my job in winter to assemble the pastry-making equipment in the warm kitchen — the right mixing bowls and spoons, the right sugars, fats and flours, the pastry board and the rolling pin. In the afternoon, a similar process might be followed to make cakes for tea — with her tiny family, and using bought bread, EMJ did not have a regular baking day, but made fresh things as needed. Tea was usually from 5.30 to 6pm, so that we could hear the weather forecast, and begin that lifelong custom of hearing it without taking in what it says. There would be bread and butter, jam and cheese, and perhaps some other spread, and two or three sorts of cake or biscuit. None of this was too much for people who were working like CWJ and EMJ, but of course it turned me into a little fatty.

The evening might bring some fruit, around Christmas time some chocolates and nuts, some toffee if we had just made some, or, as I grew older, perhaps a drink.

Life became a little more comfortable with the arrival of electricity, in the late autumn of 1951. Why was I at home? Perhaps it was half-term, or perhaps I remember several Saturdays. Two men came to do the wiring inside the house and I was there when they did the bedrooms. The wires ran neatly along the surfaces to the plugs and switches. In the bedrooms there were clever pull-switches over the bed and you could turn the light off and on at the door and in bed. Fancy not going to bed by the light of a single candle any more! Even I who always had the best CWJ and EMJ could find, only had a sweet little carrying oil-lamp which gave about the same light as a candle and had a little white funnel designed to look like a candle. On the landing and staircase, there was even a three-way switch — one switch by the bathroom which was pretty near the spare room, one between my parents' room and mine, and one at the bottom of the stairs. I didn't know electricity was so clever.

CWJ bought several things in anticipation of the great day: a television, a small portable heater, an iron and a kettle. Each room had a light bulb dangling on a cable — well, that's what we had then. There was an electric cooker too, and an immersion heater, so that EMJ could cook and have hot water in summer without having the fire burning all the time.

The lights and power went into all the buildings as well — a single bulb here and there, not brilliant light. High up on the house wall, so you could only reach it with a ladder, was the outside light, a powerful bulb which could be switched on and off in the house and in the dairy. It made evening milking easy after dark, by not having to carry two buckets of milk and a flashlight across the yard.

As it turned out, electricity didn't actually arrive until February 1952. EMJ was unwell and staying with relatives, and CWJ and I watched the television, fascinated by the King George VI's funeral procession and the opera *Rigoletto*.

The garden gave us all great pleasure, and also hard work. As soon as there was a bit of warm weather in the spring, I would be out in the vegetable garden with a fork, knowing that any digging I did would be useful. CWJ would do some too, and taught me the proper way to dig along a row. Every now and then there would be a bonfire for weeds. Then — thank goodness — one of the farm men would be sent to finish off the digging, and CWJ, with my 'help', would set the garden. There would be radish and lettuce and spring onions for summer teas — and we would pull a radish out of the ground, rub it clean, and eat it without bothering to go inside to wash it. There would be serious quantities of carrots and potatoes and beetroot (which I never cared for) and a little later lots of peas and beans. CWJ didn't care for broad beans, and EMJ's mother didn't like parsnips, so these were never grown. Later on, there would be broccoli, cauliflower, sprouts and cabbage, and strangely enough, the vegetable garden produced sweet peas, rhubarb, raspberries, currants and gooseberries, and, as weeds, lots of Flanders poppies; their seed dispersal method always fascinated me.

The flower garden was on the shady, northern side of the house, so started off with a disadvantage. But it was big enough for most parts to get some sunshine, and there were shade-tolerant plants even then for the darkest parts. The year began with a magnificent show of snowdrops, and later daffodils, under the elm tree. Then there were purple polyanthus, which I called 'damson-flowers' — and then things seemed to come in a rush. One sign of summer was the marvellous old dark-red cottage peony, which might have over 20 blossoms a year; another was the buddleia tree, which attracted hosts of butterflies; another was watering the garden on summer evenings, carrying as heavy a load as you could manage. Then we had to mow the lawn — quite a small area, or rather, three small areas. Later, we had a rotary mower, and pushing that was harder. I couldn't even start the motor without help. There wasn't much garden machinery then — at least, we didn't have much. Now, people have rotovators and sit-on mowers. But doesn't gardening involve getting soil under your finger-nails? What we had, even the forks and rakes, were kept in the old disused outside lavatory, which was decently surrounded by snowberry bushes so no-one could have seen you approaching in Victorian days.

There was an old orchard, where there were some cider apples, too sour to eat, a Tom Put tree, a greengage and a couple of Victoria plums, almost too old to bear. There were also two damson trees, and, nearer the house, a Devonshire Red with lovely glowing red apples which we used in blackberry and apple pies.

As I grew up, it was evening milking I saw most often. After the long, hard-working days of harvest, the best thing a child could do was keep out of the way, so it's winter milking I remember best. It was dark and Rusty and Beryl Pinches may have come to play with me — I suppose we were about 11, 10 and 8. Bill and Harry would do the milking, the cowhouse lights would be on and also the yard light. When either of the men slipped off to somewhere really dark, perhaps to feed the young stock, we followed. We imagined that we were silent trackers, completely hidden by the dark, but of course we were giggly children easily visible to eyes accustomed to the gloom. We would follow the men at their work and as they finished, either play in one of the buildings, never noticing the cold, or go into Bill's cottage and listen to the Archers and perhaps have a game of draughts after Bill had had his tea.

The cottage kitchen would shock people today. Initially water would have to be got from the pump. There were no fitted cupboards or fridge, just an earthenware sink, a draining-board and a stone floor. There was no television in the cottage and no bathroom either. I remember Lucy deciding one day to wash her hair. She set an enamel bowl on the kitchen table with a towel spread underneath, and fetched warm water from the blackened kettle that was always on the fire. Rusty said she'd help ('You could see I'd be going into one of the caring professions', she said years later). We couldn't find any shampoo. 'Never mind' said Rusty, and improvised with Persil from the back kitchen. Lucy, with her head in the water, didn't know. I was half admiring and half shocked.

Before water was laid on, there used to be a gathering round the pump each evening as the men fetched two buckets of water each. These would stand in the back kitchen with covers on them to keep out dust and insects and would last a normal day for drinking, cooking and washing. Wash day was a different matter, with a fire to be lit and water heated in the copper in the wash house, which stuck out at the back of the cottage together with a wood and coal store.

Summer evenings were fun too. We'd be outside as much as possible — more of a necessity for children from cramped cottages than for me. Late on in the evening, there might be a game of cricket played on the road. The crease was a little hollow dug in the road (which only consisted of small stones tightly packed in mud), the wicket a rusty old oil-can, the bat and ball old ones given by someone. All the boys would play, of course, and the younger married men from the cottages. Little girls were allowed to play (at least to field) but big girls and women would not want to join in. Every now and then someone would shout 'Car coming' and we would all leap into the ditch in a panic, someone clutching the old oil can as the car inched past.

Neighbours, especially in country districts, expected to co-operate and help out in emergencies. A note in CWJ's diary, 'Fetched Dr to Mr Thomas' (April 1931), is just one example of several that continued earlier family practice.

When CWJ and EMJ moved to Aldon, they found that the threshing machine, which was essential where there was corn to thresh, had a tight programme of work, moving from farm to farm. When it arrived in Aldon, two men came with it — no-one had a big enough work force to staff it up entirely, so men were 'lent' to and fro for half a day, a day or even two whole days. When the machine was thundering away in our top stackyard, driven by a belt from a tractor and with sweating workers feeding in the corn sheaves and taking away either bales of golden straw or sacks of corn or sacks of chaff, I was told to keep well away. 'They're busy and you'd only be in the way. Don't go anywhere near unless Daddy's there'.

Whilst the hamlet of Aldon was tiny, there were other neighbours a mile or less distant, and somehow I was more comfortable with them than with people who lived in towns or villages. In the other farm at Aldon lived the Bradleys. They left shortly after the Second World War started and their place was taken by Mr and Mrs Norris. After the war, they left and in came Mr and Mrs Jarrett and their large family. Aldon's one smallholding had been rented by a family called Morris. There were three children older than me and one younger. When they left, the smallholding was taken by Mr and Mrs Pinches. Their son and daughter and family of three girls came to live in one of Jarrett's cottages and Jack Pinches worked on his farm. Other members of the Pinches family came to live nearby.

Close by, the Pughs were settled at Aldon Court Farm when CWJ and EMJ arrived. To me, a child of the motor-car generation, the way to their house was a long way down the lane and up their long driveway. The Pughs' children loved to visit the newcomers and had soon worn a path through the fields and over a stile, a way shown to me, but I never used it. They, and especially Mrs Pugh, were strong Methodists and mainstays of the Primitive Methodist Chapel at Brand Hill, only a couple of miles away. Mr Pugh had a car, rather a ramshackle old one, but he was ready to give and take lifts and it was to him that CWJ would turn in times of breakdown or other emergency. The war probably prolonged that sort of interdependency and mutual support for a decade but it was on its way out, in exchange for closed doors, closed gates and closed cars.

As a child I used to meet Mr Pugh walking about the lowest fields with his prized Hereford bulls, training them for showing. Terrified as we children had been of bulls, we didn't mind his at all, especially if he was there, because Herefords were so quiet. Although as a small child I was frightened of all men except CWJ, I wasn't much frightened of Mr Pugh, who was nice and clean-looking. Once on the bus on the way back from a Sunday School trip, he held me up as I slipped sideways in my seat and fell asleep across the gangway. I couldn't be afraid after that, could I?

At the Jarretts' farm there were seven children when they came, from the 14-year-old daughter who was the eldest to the baby who was perhaps three years younger than me, or about one. Another boy was born later, sadly with Downs Syndrome. The oldest girl and a boy (aged about 12) were already working pretty well full time in the home and on the farm. Then there were two girls, whose job for the present was to look after the younger ones, sometimes including me, and two boys, Keith and Leslie, either side of me in age. Keith was later to farm Lower Aldon Farm. Then there were the three Pinches girls, Betty, Rusty and Beryl. What riches! I hardly noticed Mick Williams, the adopted son of Mrs Pinches at the smallholding, but he was a big boy, nearly old enough to leave school.

There were other neighbours too. Jimmy Brown and Mrs Brown lived at Stoke Wood Farm, across two of our fields. When they retired, the tenancy went to my Uncle Dennis, CWJ's half-brother. There was also Mrs Edwards and her son Len in a cottage there. Other children were frightened of her but I'd been there with CWJ and knew she was nice. She often gave me apples.

Down in Aldon Gutter was a smallholding at Withersley. Recently I have been told that this was probably the mill mentioned in the Domesday Book at Aldon. When CWJ and EMJ came to Aldon, there was a little family still there — Tom Jacks, Mrs Jacks and their daughter Phyllis, although others had married and left. How strange to find another family called Jacks almost next door! But it is not an uncommon name in this border area. Tom Jacks worked for CWJ at Aldon for a time and when he stopped, his daughter Phyllis came. Not only that, her son Tom came as soon as he left school. In the meantime, old Tom Jacks had been killed in an accident with the threshing machine.

This other Jacks family lived over half a mile from Aldon down a very steep lane. They used to milk a few cows and Phyllis had the job, every morning, of pulling two churns, one full and one only part full, up the very steep bank. Pump Bank we called it. By the time she worked for us, after the war, she had a very bad back and wore some

Life at Aldon just before Phyllis left

kind of special corset. I liked Phyllis, broad and old-fashioned though she was, but I was a bit scared of her.

Many people wanted work, especially of a part-time or short-term nature. After getting established and known, CWJ had no difficulty in finding married women and older children to lift potatoes and undertake other tasks. He would note in his diary who had done so many hours:

September 1947
Tues 30   Potatoes. Mrs Davies 5 hrs, Mrs Selley 4, Jim 2.

It was only before he became known locally that EMJ, and Clara, Dennis's wife, had to turn out and do it. I can only remember once helping to lift potatoes and it was probably a special arrangement, the last year they were grown as a field crop. In general CWJ hated growing labour-intensive crops such as beet and potatoes, preferring to do the work himself, not manage others.

Then there were Mr and Mrs Davies at Step-aside Farm in Onibury. We passed it and waved hundreds of times, but sometimes we had a chance to speak to them. They had one, youngest, daughter still living at home and known by the odd nickname of 'Bobbin'. Mrs Davies would come to visit sometimes, driving a little green rounded Morris Minor. We had to run and find an ashtray as she smoked heavily. Her hair was very white except for a yellow streak in front where the cigarette smoke stained it. Mr Davies was a small man who looked as though he had worked until he was nearly all used up. When he died, Mrs Davies stayed in the house, and another daughter and son-in-law came to live with her. That couple had twin daughters, and one of them eventually married my cousin from Stoke Wood Farm.

I remember going there one light evening to a tennis party where it was the grown-up people who made up doubles and played tennis. What sophistication!

Another 'local' family were the Locks, a gypsy family who lived in our part of the country and came round on periodic visits. I didn't know where they put their caravans and ponies when they came to Aldon, but every now and then the word would go round: 'The gypsies are about' and we would shiver in our shoes. They came to the yard door, knocked and waited politely. When EMJ came to the door, Mrs Lock would ask politely if she had a bit of bacon to spare, or anything to eat. Or some old clothes, 'all your things are so good and so smart', she would cringe. EMJ would have been planning for some time what to give them, and eventually she would go and get it. Mrs Lock brought her daughter, Sheila, a few years older than me, and totally deaf. EMJ was always touched by her and gave generously. The deafness (or, as we said then, 'being deaf and dumb') ran deep in the family. Years later I came across old Dummy Lock (William), also 'deaf and dumb', but at 80 or so quite able to walk between Bishop's Castle and Clun carrying a wardrobe.

It was also good to get out and explore the area around. There were three bicycles in our backyard — a man's cycle with a crossbar and back-pedal brakes, which CMJ could ride, my little cycle, and a new women's bicycle for EMJ, which later I used to share. 'After all' EMJ said to CWJ, 'you can use this bicycle as well. You can manage quite well *without* a cross-bar.' We didn't cycle much anyway — the lanes were too steep.

I never knew about gears and further advances in bikes. I officially stuck at not being able to mend a puncture, and I'm still ashamed of it. My cousin Michael, staying with us in the school holidays, explained to me how the gears worked on his bike at home, and how

With my little cycle

these would have enabled him to cycle up *this* bank, but not up *that* one. While he was with us he seemed quite happy to use a share of the gearless woman's bike without a crossbar.

Going to catch the bus when I went to the High School was an everyday ride, except in very extreme weather. Bicycles stood all day in an enclosed patch of ground at Haynes's Corner, ready to be pushed back up the hill after school. I was lucky enough to have a lift very often, with the bike in the back of the Land Rover. Sometimes CWJ wasn't able to pick me up, and then it was frustrating to be passed by another motorist, obviously thinking 'I needn't stop. Her Dad'll be along soon.' No-one bothered about throwing a cycle in the back of a van or a Land Rover, or pushing it into a boot.

CWJ and EMJ's first car was a second-hand Austin 7 (EJ 2714), bought in December 1931 when they had not long been at Rorrington. This was always said to belong in fact to EMJ because she withdrew her superannuation money from teaching and spent it on the car. She always thought that it was when you were young you needed a bit of cash, rather than when you were old. Having a car immediately meant they were no longer locked in the long valley between Shrewsbury and Montgomery. So, as well as doing the deliveries for the Shop, the second-hand Austin 7 went to Welshpool and to Shrewsbury, and made visits to family homes at Wotherton and Worthen. The diaries often record journeys such as 'to P.... in new car', 'took E through Middleton'.

CWJ and EMJ
outside 32 Wotherton

After the car, there came a van. The diaries don't give a date for when the first van was bought, but it was before January 1935 since that was when it was fitted with a new gasket. The following year there was an accident with the van, resulting in the purchase of a replacement in September 1936. In 1938 an Austin 10 green van was bought. Very few of the lanes had asphalt surfaces in those days so cars and vans had to do their best on hard-core and earth tracks with a strip of grass and weeds growing up the middle. I can remember plenty of lanes like that from my childhood in the '40s so there must have been even more in the '30s.

In December 1933 CWJ and EMJ went by car to see Renee and Fred in Colchester. Whilst travelling, they had asked the way to 'Bicester' but no-one could help. After a while someone said 'Bister' and that solved the problem. They were even able to have a couple of trips to London. The weather was cold and they came back driving slowly and carefully on black ice. When they got out of the car, they couldn't stand up, although the journey had been done safely enough.

A long stream of cars followed these first ones, usually lasting for a year or two before a new one was bought. They were all second-hand

Esther, K, (schoolfriends) and myself dressed ready to go shopping in August 1949 in the Rover 16

cars after the Second World War and CWJ was never able to persuade EMJ to learn to drive, even when there was no driving test.

The first one I can remember was a Vauxhall, which had a bench seat in the front. It had been bought in 1939, before I was born, and it lasted through the war until it was sold in August 1945. The next one was a Rover 16, a splendid green car with a long bonnet, running-boards and the shape of the spare wheel in relief on the lid of the rather small boot. Inside, there were dark green leather-covered seats, shiny from much use: bucket seats in front. The doors closed with a quiet, expensive-sounding click. Once, as a small child, I had a finger shut in the door, but it was quite all right afterwards, probably because of the expensive insulation inside the steel. This car stole CWJ's heart so he was never really happy afterwards with anything but a Rover, and that old lady was probably the loveliest car we ever had; before he died he had had three more Rovers.

By the time that I learned to drive I had a choice — a big car with an awkward column-based gear lever, or a Land Rover, slightly primitive with no heating and only hand-operated windscreen wipers. The Land Rover was short and would do anything — tow heavy weights and drive on slippery surfaces. The driver and passengers were high up and could see over the hedges. There was room for three adults in the front, and the dogs, or a bale of hay or some sacks of feed, in the back. We enjoyed it a lot. I learned to drive the old Land Rover round and round a field, following the wheel marks in the grass until I could do two or three laps and only leave one set of marks. When I had more difficulty reversing, I was set to reverse round and round the farmyard and in and out of the gate. I never learned to tow or reverse with a trailer full of livestock and I always thought reversing the trailer up to a narrow opening must be quite tricky. When I was in the sixth form at school and taking my driving test, we had a big Austin Princess, a heavy car with three forward gears and two overdrive gears, which you engaged by pressing and releasing the accelerator in gears two and three. Great fun, I thought, to turn the old crate into a nippy car. I could never quite get CWJ to see it like that, although he was pleased that I was turning into a keen driver. EMJ, too, liked my driving — 'she goes so smoothly and corners so well'. What fun, when I had passed my test, to take a car to school and park with the mistresses.

Passing your driving test meant that you were allowed to drive a tractor too. The men, with no need of a car licence, would simply take a tractor driver's test. Children on farms learn to drive tractors at the age of 13 or so, going round and round a field at harvest-time with some fairly basic implement. I've done that too and I know how cold it can be, even on a July afternoon. Of course, it can be very hot as well with a burning sun. CWJ would soak up the sun like a lizard. He also claimed that sitting on hard tractor seats in the cold and damp, twisting to the right to watch the furrow he was ploughing, gave him arthritis in his right hip.

Having a car meant being able to travel on holidays. First CWJ and EMJ went to visit relations at a distance, then they took me along too. One year I thought we'd invented a new sort of holiday, intending to go and stay in B&B places and driving in the day. But now I suspect that they had the idea from somewhere else! We'd planned to go to Lynton and Lynmouth in Devon, on to Cornwall, back to Auntie Renee's, and finish up at the Farnborough Air Show. At school I caught mumps and measles, so we had to put off starting. Just as well, or we would have been there on the night of the Lynton floods of 1952. By the time we eventually got away we also missed the Farnborough Air Show, which again was perhaps just as well for we also missed a spectacular crash which killed some people. My illness was quite lucky.

The next summer we set out up Scotland to go to John O'Groats. After that, it was East Anglia, and then filling in the bits in between. No-one went abroad for holidays in those days — at least, no-one of our clan — but these were quite enterprising holidays — and still the visits to relations went on.

The car and the Land Rover also meant that it was a positive pleasure for CWJ to make the school run with me day after day. To start with, vehicles were less reliable — the radiator might boil — if it was sunny there might be a note in the diary 'Fetched Diane in Lorry'. Often he would be late, delayed by work and slow travel so the boarders at school had come out from their tea at 5.45 before he arrived. I didn't mind, so long as I could get home and be comfortable. It was the same later at the High School — EMJ knew I didn't eat much of the lunch, so she used to keep me a plateful of dinner (meat, potatoes and vegetables) in what I used to call 'Dinner for Tea'. Delicious.

During the war, and in the time of austerity afterwards, there seemed to be no great shortage of travel. Of course, farmers had 'agricultural' petrol, and CWJ used the car as a taxi for the neighbours, meeting trains, etc. There were journeys to auctions in Shrewsbury or to pick up batches of new day-old chickens, and regular deliveries of eggs for sale, and somehow all the journeys managed to come back via Wotherton and Worthen. The whole journey would often be accomplished without seeing another vehicle, and black-out meant darkness. One journey in February 1942 was enlivened when the car broke down by the Bow House farm near Lydham. The neighbour, Mr Pugh, eventually came to the rescue, and towed the car back home. Having got the car home CWJ was up all night tending a cow, Queenie, as she delivered a bull calf. The following day Mr Pugh was still helping, towing the broken-down car to Shrewsbury; it was three weeks before CWJ was able to record in his diary that the car was back in working order.

Friends and relations alike were delighted to visit a farm during rationing, because there were always rabbits, vegetables, and a bit of bacon at least. So it was that my cousins from the south were visitors. Both were later in the RAF; one was stationed in north Shropshire, and not only came himself but brought a friend. Later, Cousin Peter caused great excitement by flying over our farm with the wheels of his plane down as though it was about to land — something we were told was strictly forbidden.

How lucky I was, I thought, to have two aunts (my mother's sisters) living at the seaside, one at Aberdovey and one at Pwllheli, both of whom took what we then called 'paying guests'. The journey to Pwllheli, where the paddling was best, was thrilling. Nellie, the sister who lived here with her daughter Gwen, had had a hard life. She had trained as a nurse in Shrewsbury just after the First World War, and married a patient who was a farmer in north Shropshire. He had fought in the Middle East, and was never really well after he came home. After they had been married for a while he died of an enlarged heart. She then moved to a smallholding with her son and daughter (I think she had already lost a baby boy). Richard, the son, died quite suddenly after a fall which didn't seem very serious.

Nellie then moved to Pwllheli to take in paying guests, some short-term and some long-term. Every time we visited there was a new little

My first donkey ride, Abergavenny, September 1945

girl, a 'friend' for me to play with. Not only was there the beach, the roads were quiet enough for my fairy cycle to be great fun, and there was a playground with swings, a roundabout, and even a slide! Nellie was always generous and good at giving presents. They didn't have to be expensive — I remember some grape hyacinth bulbs. How I watched those flowers grow!

Later Nellie moved to London with her daughter and set up a B&B near Victoria station. We had some good times with her, but we weren't always in her good books. Once, when I was a student in London, CWJ and EMJ came to pick me up at the end of term and stay with Nellie for a few days. Her reception was hostile, so EMJ refused any food and we set off for home the next morning. 'In future' said CWJ 'we must remember to bring an old hat and throw it in the room to her first to see what kind of reception it gets.' Gwen married and then divorced, and she and Nellie came back to Shropshire to live.

Aberdovey was within day trip distance, and didn't really have much of a beach compared to Towyn; on the other hand, my uncle worked on the railways there, and was responsible for a signal-box with gleaming brass. It was a treat to see the heavy levers which

CWJ's sister, Agnes

controlled the points, and hear the ringing of the bell which told that a train had passed a certain point on the line and would be with us soon. Everything worked like clockwork, to our great admiration.

CWJ's sister (and EMJ's school friend) Agnes married a sergeant in the British Army of the Rhine, Matthew Causer. They had two children, a boy a few months younger than me, and a girl a couple of years younger still. I got to know them first when she came home from Germany and came to keep house for me and my father while my mother was away at the seaside seeking for a cure for her asthma. I was just over seven. At least I had the sense to keep my mouth shut and not worry anyone, because Aunty Ag didn't do things properly — that is, not the same way as EMJ.

During these few weeks I learned a lot about sharing and being part of a bigger family. What fun the children had together, and what fun Michael and I had, being almost the same age. But I was terrified of my strict aunt and uncle. They were hard on their children, and I was a timid little thing, and so glad that my dear gentle father was left with me. Later on I was to find out that EMJ disapproved of Agnes punishing her children by 'hitting them across the side of the head.' Michael half-boasted that his father, whom I disliked a lot, kept a cane especially for him. They were nice normal children, clever, very musical, and Michael at least enjoyed sports. They also had a Monopoly set, which I loved, but which would have been no use to me because I had no siblings to play with. They lived in Donnington, a new town in East Shropshire, and sometimes on a Sunday evening, coming home after taking some of the family back from a weekend, I would cry from loneliness in the back of the car.

One interesting family custom is the way we spoke of couples in the family. If the man was a relative, he was *always* first — Alf and Kath, Edward and Bessie. If the woman was the relative, either might be first — Fred and Renee or Renee and Fred, Tom and Amy or Amy and Tom — unless it was a late marriage (in the sense that we hadn't had much time to get used to it) or we disliked the man, in which case he was second — Doris and Edward; Ag and Matt. Our family gave us quite a large sample to work with.

Lizzie and Katy kept on the family home at Victoria House in Worthen into the 1940s, but suddenly it looked as though the small-holding and house were going to be bought up and themselves thrown out. Grandfather and three daughters lived there then. 'Send for Cuth' said Grandfather. He understood the situation at once and immediately saw the vulnerability of these members of his wife's family who had already gone through bankruptcy in the 1920s. After a little consideration CWJ and EMJ agreed to buy the place and let it to them as sitting tenants.

Lizzie needed no advice on her garden or her bees. I was fascinated by these strange creatures, and as a toddler I called them 'buzzlings'. She said she had been stung so often that she no longer felt the stings, but EMJ shuddered.

The death of my Grandfather from Victoria House is the only time in my life I've been to a proper funeral, with the will read afterwards. I wasn't allowed to go to the service in case I found it too upsetting, but afterwards we sat round the kitchen and someone read the will. It was probably a solicitor, because the Colleys always liked to do things properly, and in novels it is the solicitor who reads the will. I noted that although EMJ was just one among several daughters, she was left the silver spoons. Later, when I asked her where we would get them from, she laughed and said 'I expect they went long ago,' meaning at the time of the bankruptcy.

When I was a tiny child, I was often confused by which war was meant when I heard CMJ and EMJ mention it. Often they meant the one which had shadowed their childhoods and brought death to many of the young men they knew. But often they meant the war which they had just come through, which had touched every aspect of their lives and which still had a powerful effect in 'Austerity'. As I grew older, I understood better.

They saw plenty of Mrs Rottan, the mother of Squire Allcroft and Miss Allcroft, who was helping to manage the estate while he was ill. She was hard-working and generally well-liked (although CWJ was never going to like anyone much if he had to pay them rent). They both preferred to pay for something outright and have free use of it afterwards but this was not possible with land in their early days. Mrs Rottan liked this young couple.

When evacuees came under discussion, Mrs Rottan said, 'Lancing College boys' school is coming to the Court. If you'd rather have evacuees from Liverpool that's all right. But if you'd rather have a master from the College just leave it to me!' So they did. She even lent them some furniture for two rooms, a living-room and a bedroom. The living-room had two armchairs which would, if necessary, turn into rather narrow, uncomfortable beds with mattresses rather like futons. There was a little oil stove, and big wooden shutters for black-out. They were to have access to the kitchen and share the new bathroom (many wartime arrangements were much more troublesome than this).

In due course, the College arrived and the master and his wife, Mr and Mrs Saw, and their Dalmatian dog, came to Aldon. EMJ didn't like animals in the house especially dogs, 'dirty things' she said 'licking their bottoms one minute and the next minute wanting to lick my hands!' But this was a special case and at least Dalmatians look nice and clean. She soon found out that this one was not very bright. If it came to her, she only had to whistle to it like its mistress did, but faintly, and off it would go.

Mr and Mrs Saw had the end room and the bedroom above it and could use the front door to come and go privately. This must have been especially useful in the first few months before the bathroom was installed, when they had to use the outside lavatory. The big downstairs rooms were too big to heat with limited supplies of coal so the tiniest room was used in the evenings. There was a small table where you could eat a meal, a fireplace, two armchairs on each side of the fire, the radio, a mat on the stone-flagged floor and blackout curtains, and that was it. Oh, and two candlesticks on the mantelpiece. Cosy evenings, with the news and radio programmes, then upstairs to bed. That was pretty bleak in winter but no-one expected heating in a bedroom, there was a chamber pot under the bed and EMJ was still using it many years later.

Despite the upheaval, my parents and the College were very lucky over the evacuation and they all knew it.

The College boys had the run of a lot of the woods and did straightforward jobs like sawing wood. I'm not sure why no-one made more use of their labour in term time — perhaps because they were too busy and were fully committed to work camps in the summer — but there is no mention in the diaries of them helping even with potato picking.

Mr Saw used to laugh about the boys' nicknames and say how glad he was that no-one could make a nickname for him. Secretly, CWJ and EMJ laughed because, as soon as they noticed him, the boys would chant very quietly, 'eeeee, eeeeee' like a saw cutting through wood. The Saws came regularly for term-time and left for school holidays, according to the diaries. Later on in the war, it is not clear to me whether they stopped coming, or whether it was so routine that CWJ stopped writing it down. After the war CWJ and EMJ moved in to the big end bedroom which the Saws had used.

Wartime and the War Ag (War Agricultural Committee) demanded the ploughing of meadows and the growing of crops which were not very familiar, and were awkward for hill farmers: sugar beet and beans as well as potatoes, swedes and mangolds. They were much-hated crops, requiring labour-intensive hoeing and ridging, hand pulling and picking and sorting. At first it was difficult to find anyone local to help with this on a piece-work basis. In disgust, EMJ and Dennis's wife Clara turned out to work in the fields, and one of the family came to stay and help. Even Dennis worked overtime in the fields in the light evenings. There was no overtime for CWJ, who simply had to work harder, which apparently was the way a lot of the wartime agriculture targets were met.

In November 1940 CMJ called out to EMJ: 'Just get your Wellingtons and a coat, and come out into the Cow Pasture.' In silence she did so. There was no child in the house to listen for before going out, and it was a clear night. They went through the garden, past the brooder houses and through the wicket by the purple lilac into the field. Then they turned south and walked a few paces in the direction of Ludlow. Not a light showed anywhere, but the 'high-reared head of Clee' was a clear landmark on that cloudless night. 'There it is. Coventry. Or what was Coventry. See the orange glow?'

It was the remains of the city still burning nearly 24 hours after the attack.

This was the closest the war had yet come, but more was to follow. One morning, coming in to bait, CWJ said 'Pop your coat on and come outside with me.' Outside was the shell of an incendiary bomb. It had been dropped during the night and burnt itself out where it fell in the yard. Fortunately, no sparks had ignited the hay which was packed into the buildings around the yard. I never found out what the enemy had been aiming for, but the north-south railway line apparently carried important ammunition between Shrewsbury and Hereford. Just before the war, a new section of the A49 had been built to carry traffic round Church Stretton, and this was used during part of the war as a kind of arms dump. Either of these might have been the target.

As soon as possible, CWJ and EMJ stopped growing beet and potatoes, feeling that both had proved that they were not ideal crops for the ground in question. Even after the required quantity of potatoes had been sent off, there might well be complaints from officials about the quality. Later, as implements improved, a lot of good quality potatoes were grown around Bishop's Castle.

You could still get deliveries at home after the war, although not as easily as earlier in the century. The Co-op used to deliver twice a week. We had three loaves of bread each time they came, two white and one brown (for me) and sometimes tomatoes. The Co-op van also went to our men's cottages to deliver groceries and to take in exchange the cheque CWJ paid them in wages each week and give them cash as change, 'What an excellent service,' I thought.

EMJ arrived at Aldon expecting as good a service from the village shop as they had provided in Rorrington. As the shop sold meat, she ordered some. The first week it was fatty and underweight. The second week it was again underweight, and was wrapped around a large lump of fat. She called the delivery man in and took him to the scales she had used at the shop at Rorrington and showed him that the actual weight was less than that shown on the bill. By this time he was gibbering to be allowed to go back to his boss. 'No, I'll pay you the amount on the bill this time, but we'll never have anything from your shop again.' And she didn't — I think I only went into the shop once in all my childhood.

During the war, that meant shopping in Craven Arms, 3 miles each way instead of one but a much wider selection of shops, or Ludlow, 6 miles each way but a proper town.

The other firm which delivered to us in the later '40s and early '50s was Mr Gatehouse's, the grocer from Ludlow with whom we were registered for our rations. Every other week Mr Gatehouse, or Mrs Hughes, the assistant, would ring up for the order. It would be given over the phone and the next day it was delivered, beautifully packed in a cardboard box. EMJ hated to miss the ordering ritual as she tried to order everything once a month; if you missed an order, they would send you the same as you'd had the previous fortnight and it wouldn't be what EMJ would want. Before I started school, we went into Craven Arms on a Friday morning (Market Day) and otherwise as needed. Typically, we would go to Market Street first, to the paper shop, as we called WH Smith, and to Woods to sell any poultry, eggs or whatever. Anything we brought would be taken to the yard where Mrs Wood and Uncle Ernie would be feathering. CWJ knew the Woods 'boys' by name but to me they were men and therefore frightening. The shop was tiled in white and shiny dark green and sold fish as well as poultry and fruit and vegetables.

Two Mr Nicholases had shops on Market Street. One sold clothes. There was an entrance for men and a separate one for women and there was an upstairs as well. I remember the assistants used to open lots of drawers to show you items such as vests and knickers. Down the back where it was darker, there was haberdashery. I once had some pretty flowered pink and blue dress material from their shop. Then rationing ended, travel became easier and we started to shop further afield for clothes. Clothes were always important to EMJ; she loved buying nice, good quality garments and showing them off. The other Mr Nicholas had a furniture shop with a splendid grass roof sticking out over the pavement. It was virtually impossible to buy new furniture then. CWJ and EMJ's house was largely furnished with saleroom buys and antiques and a good many of the antiques were saleroom buys from Mr Nicholas. Every now and then he would follow us down the road and murmur that he had just got some second-hand pieces which might be of interest. Then we would go and look. There was a lovely couch in the kitchen and part of a big sideboard — two big cupboards and some open shelving, the whole waist-high to an adult. The top part, woodwork and a mirror simply went into one of our three lumber rooms. EMJ was still trying hard to buy furniture into the 1950s and still buying piles of rubbish at sales to get hold of a single good piece. I remember the buying of a splendid mahogany gentlemen's wardrobe with three bays of drawers and hanging space. It came to pieces for moving and with difficulty was taken upstairs and into our bedroom. But it came with boxes of junk, including wooden rosaries and old bells from a great house. In this way we acquired several old trunks and suitcases, two or three broken violins in cases and a flute. Occasionally there would be something useful like a piece of cloth which would hang on the back of a door to shut out the draughts.

There were no one-way streets in Craven Arms in those days. You parked wherever you liked. So we went by car from Market Street to Dale Street. Maybe CWJ would have business in Barclays Bank. I had one of those bright metal money boxes with different sized slots for different coins. We would certainly go to Smiths the Butcher — CWJ and EMJ were friends with old Mr Smith, young Mr Smith (Fred, with his poor health) and Mrs Smith (Brenda) who sat in the little cash office. EMJ might want me to go to Mrs Andrews, who cut girls' and womens' hair. My hair has always needed styling really well and her cuts were more along the lines of 'that's level' and 'put a clip in here', so I always hated it and usually cried. The chemist's was on Dale Street as well. The owner was a Mr Phillips and another Mr Phillips worked there; his wife did sewing for EMJ so there might be a message or something to pick up. It might be necessary for CWJ to visit Les Morris, the Agricultural Engineer, or the Post Office, or, in early days, to call on Claud Summerfield who, as coal merchant, was a very important man. In summer, it might be possible to get an ice-cream, a rare treat.

We had to fit in a visit to Mrs Battery Evans. She re-charged the farm men's wireless batteries each week and we delivered and collected them but v-e-r-y c-a-r-e-f-u-l-l-y to make sure of not spilling the acid.

Down the same street there was also a shoe shop where I started a lifetime of complaints: 'It's too small,' 'It's not comfortable', and weeping and wailing. Assistants used to get cross and tell me my feet were too big — whoever heard of a 13-year-old girl wanting a size eight? There was 'no demand'. 'Yes there is, I'm here now.' You didn't face me down easily when I was young. My feet have always been big and square-shaped. Shoes usually seemed to be narrow and pointed — all wrong. Briefly in the 1980s shoes became foot-shaped. I rushed out, ordered and bought five or six pairs, reckoning they would last me a good long time. I still have one good pair and one unworn, so they are likely to outlast me.

Every other Monday was auction day. CWJ would go to Craven Arms taking a calf or some pigs. I might go to watch. I never liked this part of farming. I hated to see frightened animals pushed around and shut in pens. The actual selling with the auctioneers' incomprehensible language was quite fun.

Or we might go to Ludlow. Some days we would start out to town, up the Clun road, maybe stopping to see Mrs Phillips, a dressmaker; she talked so hard that no-one really wanted to get caught by her although the sewing was beautiful. Further up the road was the Jukes' shop where bread that was different from the usual Co-op kind could be bought. We used to drive along Coronation Avenue and stop at the bottom of Corve Street so that we could go to Mrs Peachey's with eggs, rabbits or whatever. Sometimes we went into a little dark sweetshop kept by a Mr Williams. Then there was Mr Gatehouse, the Grocer, and opposite, a shop with lovely curved windows that sold furniture, china and, when it could get them, toys, so at least EMJ and I agreed about going in there. I remember that shop had bare wooden floors, both downstairs and upstairs. An assistant would take you round and you looked at everything to see if they had anything you wanted.

On up the road were things like the bank which were boring to a child. The wonderful Feathers Hotel was there but we thought it too grand for people like us. Much later, when I was nearly grown up, we went there for lunch one Christmastime and enjoyed it very much.

There was the ironmongers, Rickards, then a little shop which sold pikelets which CWJ and EMJ liked and I didn't, and WH Smith — newspapers and pens and stationery and books all in one small space and irresistible to me. Across the road was Boots, where CWJ used to buy cattle drenches. On we could go to McMitchells when we sometimes bought underwear or dress materials and, later, sewing patterns. EMJ had never used a paper pattern until I was about 18 and was amazed at how easy it was. Before that, she would say 'I think we'll have it like *this*' and using an existing garment as a model would cut and tack until it was right. At McMitchells you ordered a pattern and collected it a week later.

Opposite was Eileen Gerard's: too smart for us, and nearby was Bodenhams. On Broad Street, a music shop sold televisions, gramophones, records and sheet music. Again, you ordered what you wanted and collected it later. I remember having the sheet music for the *Dam Busters March* from there. Then there was a shop which sold children's clothes and toys. Also at the top of Broad Street was J P Woods, just in case you'd forgotten to get something in Craven Arms, a splendid pork butcher whose sausages and pork pies were almost as good as home-made ones.

Further on towards the Town Hall was Mr Scott the jeweller. CWJ, rushing here and there and always accident-prone, was one of those people watches try to avoid. He always had a watch or a clock with Mr Scott for repair and he used to spend a lot of his time in Ludlow talking to Mr Scott. In due course they became friends. It was nice in Scott's, with jewellery and glass to look at, as well as clocks and watches. I remember EMJ choosing herself a string of pearls there and buying for me a necklace of dark green and clear glass.

Going to Shrewsbury was a much nastier, yet fascinating experience. For one thing, it was a long way, so we had to have lunch there. For another, we only went when CWJ would be going on to an auction. He was always late back to meet us, whether for lunch or to go home. We used to meet outside Boots on Pride Hill and that was the A49 so all the cars and lorries thundered past us. I was aware that EMJ was miserable but that only made me feel worse. Eventually he would show up and we would go into the restaurant in Boots for lunch. 'Warmed up in the gravy' EMJ might say of the meat. The waitresses were poor old things in uniform and with bad feet. You tried hard not to sit at tables looked after by the slowest of them but sometimes you couldn't help it. If you had strangers sitting at your table, you opened the conversation in the good old way, 'Where are you from then?' and talked until you found places or people in common. Once when we did that, we found a man who was a distant cousin of EMJ's. Then back to the car, perhaps by way of the old market hall. We didn't buy things there but there were public toilets — very nasty ones where you had to put a penny in the door to get in and you couldn't wash afterwards. Going home and being at home was wonderful after all that.

Chapter Six

Entertainment

There were several parties and celebrations throughout the year — assorted birthday parties for us children (in large families two of the children might be grouped together and share a single party), the annual Sunday School anniversary party held in the summer at which children would perform a song or recitation in front of their parents, Bonfire Night which was celebrated on a different farm each year with a large fire and a few fireworks. In the summer there was also a School trip to the sea-side or some interesting place. After the Coronation we went to London 'to see the decorations'. What I remember is being dreadfully thirsty and not allowed to drink, presumably because nobody wanted a troop of little girls all demanding public toilets which were much harder to find then. The coach stopped by the road-side for us to be given some bread and margarine and a hard-boiled egg; we each shelled our own and ate them for lunch. No rushing into a shop to buy crisps and cola with unlimited pocket money. Other years we might go somewhere like Harlech so we could visit the castle as well as look for starfish or limpets or razor-shells.

The Sunday School trip was similar but not so educational. One year we simply went to a funfair. There were two coach-loads. Lots of mothers went, and it was a big event for many of them too. Fewer fathers went as many would be busy with the harvest. One year we went to Barmouth, and with some of the other little girls I got cut off on a sandbank by the tide. Mr Griffiths and John Pugh, both big tall men, were able to walk out and carry us back through the water that was too deep for us.

One year we were told there was going to be an Eisteddfod in Ludlow for all the Methodist Sunday Schools. There were so many things to enter for — like a kind of super Anniversary.

Miss Pugh arranged for her brother-in-law, Jack Griffiths the Coppy House, to coach us. We entered for the recitations and solos (for those who could sing) from our age groups. Then the whole Sunday School was divided up for part-singing and for choral speaking. There were other competitions as well — painting, and various crafts to be sent in advance, and others such as 'Telling a Bible Story' which had to be done on the day.

Our school failed miserably in the recitations amongst allegations that the judge had coached a good number of the entrants and that she would therefore favour 'her' pupils.

Back in Broad Street Chapel, the Eisteddfod ground boringly through the programme of events: dozens of recitations both solos and duets, choral speaking, and choirs each singing the same hymn in turn. At some point we must have gone out for tea, each Sunday School in order. When we got back, things were brisker. There were more men about, always a sign that it was getting more interesting. One of the last events was 'Telling a Bible Story: Your Own Words' and I had entered for this. It had involved a lot of work: identifying a story, writing it out, learning it by heart and saying it. But I was too young to be nervous. I was glad the Chapel was fairly full. I waited to collect my audience, and then I let go. We had been taught to make our voices carry and mine did, little though I was. Galleries and balconies and corners — they could all hear me. My story was about the birth of John the Baptist, long after his mother Elizabeth had given up hope. Why? I have no idea, except that it wasn't boring and commonplace. Not many children had entered for this unusual event, and I won first prize.

Jack Griffiths had enjoyed the coaching for the event, and so he and Miss Pugh decided to seek out other local Eisteddfodau. Two were soon found: one at Kerry (Ceri) near Newtown, and one at Kington. Programmes were obtained and passed round. They included recitations for various age-groups, but these, especially Kington, were big events with grown-ups taking part in the evening, and many prizes! Look, you could even win money prizes for the children's events! Yes, but there was an entrance charge. This was all quite new to us.

The first consideration was where to rehearse? For Ludlow we had rehearsed at the Chapel at Brand Hill or at Mrs Bennett's because she had what we called an organ (a harmonium). Mr Griffiths was looking for something different, and eventually EMJ agreed to play for them if rehearsals were in our kitchen and she could use our piano. So, once or twice a week in early summer evenings, the coach and a troop of little girls would arrive and would sing or recite. CWJ liked to listen when he could, but otherwise the only audience was the group of competitors. I dropped out of competition reciting after the experience of the heats in Ludlow, and, I think, another girl did too. This left only one specialist 'reciter' and she did her best to develop the fire and *llef* which seem to come more naturally to the Welsh.

The Eisteddfod at Kerry came first. We had to get hold of Sankey and Moody's hymns, and learn some of them. One event was for groups of four singers. There were eight of us, so there could be two groups if I agreed to sing. Naturally I was included in the younger, weaker group. Two of us had good voices and could carry a tune, two of us could not.

We set off for Kerry, CWJ driving some of the competitors in our car. I remember that we went by Newcastle-upon-Clun and over the Anchor. In Kerry, where a marquee had been set up on this Saturday afternoon, 'Lend me the money to go in — I'll pay you back later' said Rusty. So of course I did.

Inside the marquee, people sat in rows on those agonisingly uncomfortable wooden folding chairs which lurched on the uneven grass underfoot. All too soon, we had to go and sing in a foursome. The bigger girls went before us, then it was our turn. We got through to the end all right. Then the prizes. Incredibly, we had won first prize. The hymn we had had to sing was *Hark, There Comes a Whisper*. 'Very appropriate', said the adjudicator, 'they began so quietly we thought they were going to break down. But no. They were well-balanced, no one voice drowning the others ...'. So it was partly that we had been lucky with the hymn they chose. Still, it was nice to win.

Rusty must have won something else as well, perhaps a third prize or prizes. Anyway, she paid me back the entrance money and had some to spare. Later I heard EMJ say to CWJ 'Some people really are lucky. Look at Rusty, I don't suppose they saw at home that she had enough money to pay to get in, but look how much she must have won.'

The May Fair was another good source of entertainment. Polite adults, usually unable to think what to say to a child, would ask, 'Are you looking forward to the Mayfair?' It wasn't just an occasion for children; some years Bill and Harry would have a half-day holiday so they could go too. I must have been about seven and was definitely looking forward to it, although I was too timid for most of the activities. The brilliant waggons and stalls and rides were arranged on the patch of ground behind Barclay's Bank and the Methodist Chapel in Craven Arms. I can remember going round with CWJ, for EMJ hated any kind of noisy, crowded event, but he rather liked it. There were some mild and easy games — tossing rings or rolling pennies. There were roundabouts and hobby horses. As we went round in the daytime, the big rides and more difficult games would not even have started; 'Those aren't for little girls', I was told, as the dodgems and the shooting gallery were pointed out. But I was quite happy, I had had a lot of fun.

A professional photograph taken on one of the trips into town

When I was at school we were told that we must not go to the

Mayfair in case we caught infections and spread them around the rest of the children. I never went to another Mayfair until I was well into my 20s.

The harvest festivals came in early October. We naturally went to the Sunday School Chapel service, but sometimes we went to the Church service as well.

In those days, September was the month of the oats and barley harvest, especially on our top ground. Nowadays, when silaging seems to be over so soon, it's hard to remember that hay harvest used to go on into July. If you were lucky with the weather, there might be a short break between the hay and the corn harvests, and we used to comment that 'They've started combining the Earl of Plymouth's corn [on land near Ludlow], and it's only the twenty-somethingth of July.' That seemed really early to us.

The Chapel would be decorated for the Harvest Festival. We — a mixture of Sunday School children and older helpers — would go on the Saturday before the service specially to do the decorating. There would be lots of fruit, leaves, flowers, and whatever else had been given. The whole place smelled wonderful — that marvellous autumn chrysanthemum smell. There wasn't that much room for the decorations however: two sloping window sills, the railing round the pulpit, the little organ (but it still had to be usable), the stove, if it wasn't to be lit, and some of the coat hooks. But we worked hard and had a wonderful afternoon, which I enjoyed far more than I did the service the next day when the men, present in unusual numbers for a Chapel service, would thunder out:

> Some is safely gathered in
> Ere the winter storms begin.

Of course, since the corn harvest started later than it does now, it usually finished later too, and was rarely over before October. The man of a household, out and about in the fields and on the roads, would be watching how others were getting along and would come in and report, 'I see so-and-so's finished harvest.'

What could be more magical for a child than Christmas — especially Christmas for a child who read Alison Uttley? There was a lot to do — buying presents, cards and decorations, special plays and parties and services, at school and at home, preparing special food, putting up decorations, and family visits.

EMJ always said she liked to do things in a rush at the end, as we trailed into Ludlow looking for presents. 'It feels more like Christmas if it's a rush.' Of course, I just wished I didn't have to take part. EMJ was difficult to shop with for a present because she would always stop to consider whether the recipient would like it. If not, it didn't matter if *we* liked it, we'd have to go on.

The same applied to birthday cards, Christmas cards and post-cards. It was years before I learned to buy the number I needed, plus a few spares, of what I liked and send them out. Even now, I always insist on a separate pack of cards for people whose tastes differ a lot from my own.

EMJ used to play a kind of game with the Christmas cards. She would buy an assortment and write a label for each recipient. The cards would be spread out on the kitchen table and every other surface, and a label placed on each card. These would be moved depending on a number of factors, such as 'So-and-so likes this kind of picture and verse' and 'X will visit Y over Christmas so I can't send them both the same card.' Eventually it was done, and she only had the cards to write and the envelopes to address. She sent about thirty cards and I sent fewer. Some years, there were prizes and presents for guests at a children's Christmas tea, or I might need presents to take to a party I had been invited to. Some years I liked the presents for other children so much that EMJ let me keep them, while she quietly bought something else to send. I did appreciate being spoiled — not just the money but the love too. I've only just parted with one such 'present' — a box of twenty-four crayons in lovely shades. To me they were far too precious to use, but I spent hours grouping them in exciting colour combinations and re-arranging them in their box to find my favourite colour.

Parcels had to be packed, another job at which she was skilful. First, a box had to be cut and moulded to the right shape, each item wrapped in Christmas paper and placed inside, then the box wrapped in brown paper and fastened with string and sealing-wax. I knew you could buy string and sealing-wax, but it was not until I was grown up and living away from home that I found you could buy wrapping paper and brown paper. We never did — it was always carefully unwrapped and put away. There could have been no useful sticky tape either, or CWJ would have had it. He loved new things like that, whereas EMJ preferred the string and sealing-wax with which she was familiar.

Going to the Post Office, usually in Ludlow, but sometimes in Craven Arms, was another Christmas event. We took a pile of cards and presents to post and expected to have to wait a good while. And what a lot the post cost!

As for the Christmas tree, we piled into the lorry and set off across the field for the Cow Pasture. At the bottom was The Wood, more formally known as The Yelds, where the land sloped away very steeply. It had been planted by the Estate with conifers, bluebells grew underneath, pheasants roamed, and it was part of 'the shoot'. CWJ drove the lorry up as near to the trees as he could, and taking brummock and sickle, climbed on to the roof of the cab. We got out and watched, holding our breath as he cut the top off one of those trees and brought it back to the lorry. 'Don't tell anyone what we've done. It's forbidden in the tenancy agreement to fell trees.' So I never did tell, until I was grown up and felt the time for secrecy was past. The tree, some holly which one of the men would bring, and some mistletoe which CWJ would have been watching grow for some time, were brought inside on Christmas eve.

One of the most magical experiences was walking through the woods on lanes and paths with Kathleen, her sister Eileen, and John Pugh, to sing carols. Coat, hat, gloves, Wellingtons, scarf and flashlight. Someone — John? — must have spent ages working out the route. We walked for a couple of miles, stopping to sing every five or ten minutes and always welcome at those out-of-the-way houses. Our tin of money would get heavier and I quickly learned the words of the carols all the way through. John would make his little speech about collecting for the Methodist Children's Homes, but no-one cared much for that. It was 'the carol singers' they wanted and it was a real experience for them and for us. The other three could sing in tune, and even I, buzzing and squeaking along in the background, was a welcome bit of extra noise.

After an hour or so, some of it on paths strange to me, we would emerge on to the lanes at some tiny settlement, to be picked up in a Land Rover, van or large car and driven round in a larger group for the rest of the evening. This larger group would sing in villages or farms, and finally end up somewhere for cups of tea and mince pies in someone's back kitchen, where muddy Wellingtons didn't matter on the stone floor. Then we would be dropped off at home. 'See you on Thursday', because we had three nights of singing altogether.

Then, one evening, EMJ would say 'Let's get the decorations out', and I went with her into the icy-cold, unheated front hall. We opened the chest, a beautiful polished oak dower chest, and sniffed its Christmas smell. Then out came two or three boxes of decorations, folded up and put away the previous year. There were some new ones too, from that year's shopping. Back in the warm, we unpacked the boxes. Paper garlands, enough for the dining-room and the kitchen. Drawing pins. A separate box of Christmas-tree decorations. It was hard work then to get two rooms and a tree decorated by bedtime, and serve tea as usual. I had more chance than usual to do things, even if I didn't do them well, so I put up garlands, twisting them so that they would turn in the heat or a draught, and fixing them with drawing pins as I went. Never mind if the colours were all jumbled up. I put sprigs of holly behind pictures and into empty pots and vases. Someone hung up mistletoe. The Christmas tree was set up in the corner. 'Don't you want to come and help decorate the tree?' Of course I did.

There were two fairy dolls, perhaps six inches high, one with fair hair and one with dark. Both had been dressed by EMJ in crepe paper and tinsel and they had wings. The fair doll was dressed in white, the dark one in blue. Tinsel trimmed their dresses, outlined their wings which had wire frames, and made head-dresses for them. One went on top of the tree. There were only a few decorations, including a little tinsel house with Father Christmas sitting on the roof, given by one of my aunts. My special favourite was 'the bush-tail bird', a light hollow bird with pink and blue on his silvery body, and a handsome silvery-white bush tail. One year he lost his tail, and although I would gladly have kept him with my army of broken toys, he disappeared. There were candles in clip-on candle-sticks. Well, we couldn't have tree lights without electricity, could we? And we knew that candles were dangerous. I was only allowed to watch when they were lit and they were only alight for a few minutes. That meant that the candles would do for the next year too, and the next …

If people came to tea, there might be little presents for them on the tree. Otherwise, it was a good job we had plenty of tinsel, and cotton wool to make big soft flakes of snow. Even EMJ was prepared to throw away Lamda (artificial snow) although everything else, and as much as possible of that, would be saved for further years.

There was no nonsense about Father Christmas in our house. When I was about three, I announced that I wasn't going to bed that Christmas Eve. 'I'm not having some strange old man coming into my bedroom.' EMJ cracked at once and told me the truth — she always hated lying to me about anything. 'And you do understand that, all over the world, it's their Daddies dressing up and taking the presents to them?' After a warning not to talk to other children about this — 'If their parents want them to believe in a Father Christmas, it's up to them' — I could go to bed and sleep safely.

The best presents would be from my parents, but lots of others would come by post. I didn't know that there was no post on Christmas day because CWJ used to meet the postman for a few days in advance and 'hold back' presents and cards until the day itself. He did the same for birthdays too.

So on Christmas morning we had cards and presents to open in the warm kitchen. Aunts would send me books — picture books, nature books, books about children on farms, any books, apparently I never had enough books, and there were some duplicates. There would be a box of chocolates from the men, and another smaller one from Grandma who had so many to buy for. EMJ always had a box of preserved fruit from the Grocer as a kind of 'thank you' for her year's custom, and how she enjoyed it! They were not easy to find but I used to try hard after he stopped sending them. As it happened, CWJ and I weren't especially fond of them, so it was a real treat for her.

I don't remember them all, those exciting presents my parents bought, but one year I specially wanted one of those drinking ducks (a wooden toy whose head was balanced in such a way that in a warm place it was lifted and then dipped so that it appeared to be drinking from a small dish on its stand). In Shrewsbury one day each parent 'looked after' me for a while and each rejoined us looking pleased. It turned out that they had both been successful in buying ducks, so we had two. The question was 'Would the kitchen be warm enough?'. It was, and the ducks stood on the mantelpiece 'drinking' for years.

One year after the coming of electricity, but while still sleeping in my parents' room, I had a very successful year. (Perhaps I had been unwell just before Christmas, which would explain why I was still upstairs at this time of day.) The main present was an electric gramophone, with a few records. Other little presents included a travelling soap-dish with a lid for when we went on holiday and a compass with a rather wobbly idea of where North was. Now I think of it, CWJ must have done the shopping that year: the records were more to his taste, and it was like him to buy too many presents, and like her to recognise that he was good at presents and wrap them all up.

Her ideas were more practical, like a Christmas when I was nearly grown up. A lot of money had been spent on decorating and furnishing the end room, and I loved it. But although you could light a fire in the grate, it would be useful to have an electric heater. So one was bought, and as it cost over £20, it was the main present for all three of us. It lasted forty years until one irreplaceable radiant bar and the flex both went.

Once I was too old for CWJ to bother stopping the postman and saving up the Christmas post, there wasn't much excitement to Christmas day. A lovely dinner, yes, usually goose, but turkey in later years because it was so useful for post-Christmas entertaining. Real dark Christmas pudding, with both whipped cream and brandy butter, but not so nice I thought as the lighter, fruitier 'plum-ish' pudding of ordinary days At tea-time there would be the usual bread and butter and jam and cheese, followed by both Bennett's and home-made mince pies, as well as Bennett's Christmas cake. The cake was beautiful — large, perfectly round and flat and covered with white icing. A paper garland round the sides hid the dark fruit cake. Round the top edges were pink and white iced decorations, and on top was an iced message 'A Merry Christmas', and a little scene with one or two bright decorations — perhaps Father Christmas pulling his sleigh up the icing, watched by a robin. The whole thing smelled deliciously rich and spicy, but when it was cut I didn't like it much. The cake was too rich, the white icing was too hard and I didn't like marzipan. But the grown-ups seemed to find the cake a treat (and I'm sure it was after rationing) and EMJ usually made the final bits last until around Easter.

There would be a certain amount of visiting between relations and friends. I'm afraid I found the relations increasingly boring as I got older. Friends were more interesting. But at Christmas time it was 'Oh, we'd love to see you. You must come while we've still got some cake left' or 'while the tree is still up.'

First because I was too young and then because I was out at school, I was only half-aware that Christmas was made horrible for CWJ and EMJ by the pressure to pluck and dress as many chickens as possible — some two hundred or so — for the Christmas market. Most of the chickens went to JP Wood's, so what a relief it was when they opened their 'Chukie Brand' factory at the Grove in Craven Arms.

After Christmas it was back to work, with a dribble of visits and parties to enliven it. Private parties meant both taking and receiving a gift of some kind. The best party, I thought, was the Sunday School one in the old village hall at Onibury. We would arrive, leave our coats in the cloakrooms (girls to the left) and avert our eyes (mine anyway) from the disgusting lavatories. Then through into the main hall where the tea would already be spread out. As soon as most children had arrived we sat down and once everyone was there, we started. There were always plenty of helpers to see we sat down in the proper order, ate the right food and had enough tea to drink. We would start with a dish of tinned jelly or trifle (imagine trifle with no sherry and no cream!). Then there were sandwiches. My taste buds cringe at the thought of Spam. Jam sandwiches were better. Then there were cakes — big sponge cakes with jam or chocolate filling in the middle, and lots of little cakes — butterfly cakes were popular, but not with me — some with 'mock cream' on them. One taste told me I hated it — nasty slimy mess. I was not surprised to learn later after reading of wartime recipes that mock cream was made from whipped-up milk and margarine, another of my great hates.

Then there were party games. These mainly involved people standing in one or two large rings, and much rapid dashing to and fro to change places, and be in a certain place when your name was

called, like turn the trencher. The helpers stopped the incompetent —
which usually included me — making too great fools of themselves.
But one year, I suppose as I grew older, I found I was winning. One of
the competitions was easy — you had to race to eat a bar of chocolate
— my favourite! No problem there. And the prize was another bar
of chocolate! There was the usual musical chairs and lots of singing
games. One year I remember we were divided into groups and were
singing different nursery rhymes to the tune of *The Happy Wanderer*.
In my group Kathleen kept singing away, in tune and in time, as well
as cuddling the little ones and comforting the crying ones. But I had
a job too: to keep thinking of new nursery rhymes which the other
groups hadn't thought of yet, and to remember the words. I can't
remember who won, but it was good fun, even if lots of the others got
bored before I did. We never played it again.

CHAPTER SEVEN

School

EMJ gave me lessons at the kitchen table while she was cooking and ironing. I would read, write and do arithmetic. She, who was agnostic, also taught me religion. 'Haven't you taught her that yet?' horrified relatives would exclaim. But she didn't believe in telling children what they couldn't understand, just as she didn't believe in hitting a child. She never argued with you either unless you mattered a lot to her. She just went her own way quietly. So one day, while I was sitting at the kitchen table, she said 'Did you know that there was once a man who was killed, and they said he came back to life?' No, I didn't, so she explained it to me, then at school and Sunday School I learned all the Bible stories and the usual hymns and songs.

I went to Sunday School long before I went to 'proper' school. This was taught by one of the Misses Pugh at the Methodist Chapel at Brand Hill, about two miles walk from home. Everyone else must have had dinner earlier than us, because every Sunday a troop of children came to call for me at 1pm just as we were sitting down to dinner. EMJ said it was silly to start so early, as we knew the Pughs' car would overtake us and give us a lift for the rest of the way. So we finished our dinner, half-listening to 'The Naturalist' on the Home Service, with the magnificent 'Call of the Curlew'. Then we would start out, half-a-dozen or so little girls, and perhaps a few brothers with them, walking and quarrelling and arguing for a mile or so, passing our Criftins and Jarrett's Dingle, passing the stream from Spring Head, passing the steep path to Selley's (only we said 'Sealy'). Sometimes, some of the Selleys came with us. We trudged on up the road and eventually, thank goodness, we heard the Pughs' car behind us on the unmade road. It stopped and marvellously there was room for us all. Mr Pugh was driving, and Miss Pugh, who would teach Sunday School, was sitting in front with him. Sometimes they would have a young cousin with them. We piled in, younger ones sitting on the knees of older. The car was in a bad state, with holes in the floor through which you could see the grass growing up the middle of the road.

Sometimes we walked all the way, until we came to the cottages of Brand Hill and were joined by children who lived there.

The Chapel was on its own, on a straight, level stretch of road. Some people at a nearby cottage had a key and they, or someone, had lit the stove. There was no electricity, no water, no sanitation, just a single, biggish room with cream painted walls inside, a slightly sticky, bright brown paint on the rows of wooden benches with backs, the door and the raised and fenced-in platform at one end. We piled in and sat down in our natural order, boys one side and girls on the other, older children at the back, younger in front. If you were very little (say, under 5), an older girl (about 7) might look after you. Mrs Bennett played the harmonium for hymns. There was a simple little service, with opportunities for children to choose hymns. CWJ had prepared me for this. 'If you get a chance, ask for *What a friend we have in Jesus*.' So I did. But I hadn't heared Miss Pugh say 'Now you boys, choose a hymn'. They all teased me afterwards.

Then we split into classes — about three of them. I was in Mrs Bennett's class. Afterwards, the adults stayed for the proper service whilst we dashed off with a wonderful sense of freedom. Then there would be an argument — should we go back by the road we had come, or 'through the wood'? The distance was about the same but the latter route meant that some of the older girls walked part of the way with their school friends who were either going back to Onibury, or to houses 'in the wood'. So it was usually the wood — half a mile or more of lane, then footpaths and finally by the Keeper's Cottage, up a steep path through the wood at the bottom of our cow-pasture and home, legs shaking because the last bit was so steep. Going that way, we passed wonderful hazelnut and sweet chestnut trees and it was interesting to see where people lived including one of the big girls at Sunday School who had an aunt younger than herself.

Some Sundays we would be going to visit family at Wotherton and Worthen, so CWJ and EMJ would be waiting for me in the car outside

Sunday School. Soon our Miss Pugh married and another Miss Pugh took over. The oldest Miss Pugh of all had married the farmer who lived nearest to the Chapel and soon their children started to attend — five boys first, then two girls.

Considering the difficulties of large families, no water and difficult access, it is wonderful how clean and tidy everyone was. Sunday school led to a wide social life of its own — Anniversary, trip, special services for occasions such as Harvest Festival and Christmas, Carol Singing, Christmas party and scripture exams. Later there was the Guild in the evening and then children moved on to the Chapel proper.

After going to Sunday School, there was talk of the village school. I was happily doing lessons (reading, writing, arithmetic etc) at the kitchen table while EMJ worked. Her experience teaching infants at Chirbury School had made her exceptionally well qualified to teach me. I was good at it and I loved it. The problem was the walk — about one and a half miles each way up and down the hill and across a busy main road and a level crossing. 'No', said CWJ and EMJ, 'It's too much for a delicate, asthmatic child' so they went to the Education Offices in Shrewsbury and argued for a school bus. At first, the officers said no but then they agreed that the distance between Aldon and the school should be measured. Of course, it was over a mile and a bus was reluctantly approved, not for me, but because there were a lot of children who had already walked over a mile by the time they reached Aldon. The bus was immediately called 'the Dilly'.

The school consisted of two big rooms at right angles to one another. In one, Mr Purcell taught the seniors, 'Aud Perce Pig' they called him. In my room there were two classes. Mrs Purcell taught the middle class, and then there were the infants as well. Although I could read and write quite well, I was told to sit at a table and draw. The two women teachers wanted to move me up and sent me to Mr Purcell but he wouldn't accept me — he had a system of his own, based on ages and time in class.

The school meals were a shock to me. The lavatories, which were earth closets, were an even worse one. But the biggest shock of all was when two friends, about my own age, Carol Rogers who wore glasses and Mavis Harrington, with curly hair, said 'You can play with us tomorrow' but by tomorrow they had forgotten all about it. As the child of careful, older parents, I had never known that people could break promises. I only managed to attend the school for ten days or so before being ill and leaving.

'That's enough' said EMJ 'We'll pay and send her somewhere private, but she's not going back there'. So they started to look at local schools. Eventually they selected Hill House School at Culmington Manor, which was about two or three miles the other side of Craven Arms. The headmistress there believed in teaching children according to their ability, not their age, and EMJ stressed that I was a clever child.

The headmistress arranged for us to meet the Owens family who lived quite near us and whose daughter, Sheena, went to the school. There were two Mrs Owens, Sheena's mother and Grandmother. They had a little old car and Mrs Owen Junior took Sheena to school each day, so over tea it was arranged that, from September, we should meet up in Craven Arms and take it in turns to complete the journey to school. In the afternoons, the journey would be reversed. Sheena was a couple of years older than me, and would look after me.

The school had been based in the South-East, but had been evacuated to Knighton during the war after which it had taken this much bigger building with lovely grounds. As a day girl, I wouldn't need to go upstairs and as one of the youngest (I was nearly seven) I would only need to use the juniors' entrance. The classroom was a long corridor with coat hooks. We had a little locker for our lace-up and indoor shoes and a shoe bag on our coat peg for pumps and dancing shoes. Wellingtons went on wooden pegs in the boot-room which was where we also got paint-water. The lavatory was once again a bit of a shock — a water closet, but no lock on the door, so you had to pee while other people washed their hands. What a sordid business this education was. I have since learned that there was a book you were supposed to sign each day once you had 'been' as it was elegantly phrased. Thank goodness I didn't know about it at the time, and so managed to avoid it. It would have given me constipation for life.

We young ones worked in a classroom with some full-size desks and chairs and some miniature ones. There were four or five boys aged 7 or 8 and naturally they sat together at the back. We learnt French, which was new to me, and arithmetic, which I found difficult at first, and other new subjects like grammar, dictation, botany and painting. If someone wanted to go to the lavatory they raised one hand

and asked permission to 'be excused'. This quickly became the usual expression for 'going for a pee' and the girls, rather cleverly, I thought, used 'go seriously' for the next stage. School food was dreadful. We sat ten at a table, and two servers queued up for food for each person in turn. The food was served out by the ever-busy headmistress and her colleagues and was already cold by the time it reached us. Since it was basically old cow, underdone boiled potatoes with the eyes left in, and one vegetable, it didn't really matter. It was a great improvement when we had re-constituted powdered potatoes. One day a week we had a fishcake each and one day mince and rice, or mince with curry powder and rice. After reading *Kim* I decided to like even this curry.

Puddings were better, being mostly baked sponge, in which I could taste some sort of sponge mix. The worst was Monday when we had rice or some sort of milk pudding. I used to like rice at home, sweet and creamy with a delicious crisp, nutmeg-flavoured skin. But school rice was different — either milk with a few hard grains in it, or thick clotted lumps of yellowish gloop. Sago we called 'frogspawn' and tapioca was worse because of the taste, although I liked it as a savoury in later life. Even now, when two of us meet, we talk about how disgusting those Monday puddings were and how lucky you were if a friend or neighbour at table actually *liked* the stuff and would eat your share or part of it. I could not learn to choke it down, which was strange because I had already learnt to swallow school milk from bakelite beakers without tasting it.

As it was almost impossible to get any help with housework just after the Second World War, we suspected the cooking was done by the headmistress, who was always late for her classes.

Thank goodness I was at home in the mornings and the evenings. We went home to warmth, comfortable beds, good food, and later, television. What luxury! The boarders stayed for a high tea which was mostly white bread, margarine and fish-paste, tea and an evening of prayers, prep and early bed in a chilly dormitory, early rising the next day, music practice, prep, breakfast of cereal and more bread and margarine, this time with marmalade. School was nearly always cold — there were radiators, providing mild background warmth, and open fires in classrooms but not upstairs of course. In the junior classroom, the girl who shared a desk with me — another farmer's daughter, with a real talent for drawing — was so cold in class that she knitted some of those Bob Cratchett fingerless gloves and wore them in class. No-one did more than grumble because winter always meant being cold, especially when it snowed and we went out to play as usual.

CHAPTER EIGHT

Growing Up

These were the years when I was growing up and learning lots about home but also deciding that it was not for me for the whole of my life. To their credit, my parents wanted me, their only child, to be able to choose — right until I was at university they said I could come home if that was what I wanted. But they were also determined, long before school had picked it up, that I was going to university, so I might as well work hard at Latin right from the start. You had to have Latin 'O' Level to get into university in those days and we were badly taught.

Even though I started school properly at the age of six (in 1949), home, and my parents, were by far the strongest influences in my life for many years.

It's interesting recalling how and where you learnt about 'life'. When there were Belgian refugees working at Stockton during the First World War, the schoolgirl Esther, aged between 10 and 14, and one of her younger sisters came upon some items belonging to one of the refugees. 'Oh look,' said soft-hearted younger sister. 'How much he must miss his children to have these toys here.' 'Nonsense,' thought Esther. 'I know what a condom looks like if you don't.' I didn't know what a condom looked like when I was that age!

As a child I heard remarkably little bad language, and none at home. Of course, I knew 'damn' and 'blast' and 'bloody' and being Shropshire, I knew that 'bugger' was a swear word, although until I was a student I had not the slightest idea of its meaning. We used to joke because on a good day you could hear them blasting rock in the quarries at some distance — the Clee Hill for instance — and the word which we used for this was 'boarsting'. It therefore seemed logical to us that since 'blast' was a swear word so must 'boarst' be.

One older girl on a neighbouring farm started to work at home but to our pre-teen shock, outside not inside. She had an accident to her foot and was reported to our horror and secret approval to have said 'Oh my bloody toe'. Quite clever to be able to swear but be above reproach because it was factually correct.

What I managed to learn was the plain meaning of quite a lot of four-letter words, but I didn't even know that they could be used as swear words. No-one said 'Oh God' or 'Jesus Christ' much, as they do today. Among our Methodist neighbours was one family who would do no field work on a Sunday even if it was a last-minute rush to get the harvest in and rain was forecast for the Monday.

When Kenneth Tynan famously said 'Oh fuck' on television I must have been in the first year sixth at school. I didn't see the programme but a friend in the Upper Sixth told me about it on the school bus the next day.

There was at least one way in which the members of larger, younger and physically less scattered families than mine had an advantage over me. They knew more about sex and babies. Mine must have about the last and largest group to be brought up knowing little and saying less. Earlier generations, in the crowded conditions of accommodation for the working class, knew only too much. Later, in and after the 1960s, people developed a more open attitude.

EMJ's belief was always to tell the truth to a child and explain as much as you could. So, when well before school age I asked what the cow and bull were doing in the yard, she told me that the bull was going to put 'a kind of germ in the cow, and it would grow to become a calf'. I was satisfied. When I was 6 or 7 a baby boy was born at the Jarrett's and his older sisters tried to tell me that you could see the stork had brought him because you could see the seams where he was joined up. 'Rubbish' I thought, remembering the cow and the bull.

We knew we had to talk as 'properly' as we could. One day when CWJ was sitting in the winter sun on the kitchen steps to change the liners on the milking units, I asked some question about the 'tit-cups' as the men called them. 'Oh no', he said, 'if you're going to talk or write about them at school, it must be 'teat-cups'. 'Tit-cups is all right about here and with the men.' I was ashamed of not knowing.

Just after the First World War Cuth and his brother Alf were still living at home, and Grannie was worried. 'Cuth, is Alf engaged?' 'No.' 'Did he ought to be?' 'Er ... yes.' When I first heard this, I was more struck by the bad grammar than by the implication of premarital sex. I was discouraged from using slang, but I was pounced upon ruthlessly for using bad grammar. How lucky I was. 'Don't say 'spuds'', said EMJ, 'I don't like it.' I don't exactly love it myself, but it has now become a mainstream part of the language. And I couldn't help noticing that her sister Nancy said it all the time instead of potatoes, and very nasty it sounded, too.

Only once can I really remember being scolded for using bad grammar. I had been picked up from Sunday School and we were going to visit my grandmother. ' ... ... to Rusty and I', I chattered. EMJ was seriously displeased, and made me think about it.

We never said 'TV', but always 'television'. If occasionally we descended to 'telly' or 'box' it was always with an underlying joke. The plain expression at home was 'Wellingtons', but at school the children said 'Wellies', and 'goosegogs' where we said 'gooseberries'.

The television was a much more effective purveyor of popular culture than the radio. Some people had smart cabinets with doors which closed across the screen. Ours was set up first in the dining room — the best room — but quickly moved to the kitchen, which was warmer. The screen was tiny, only about 12 inches, and of course, it was black and white but it brought us Muffin the Mule, the Flowerpot Men, old films, Variety ('not much variety about it. All the programmes are the same!'), children's television and Francis Durbridge thrillers as six-part serials, and that special television culture of interludes, announcers (Mary Malcolm, Sylvia Grey, and McDonald Hobley) and the Test Card, plus whole new worlds such as archaeology and medicine and politics and panel games.

We saw lots of personalities, or celebrities as they would be called today. Unfortunately, we were too innocent to enjoy them properly. We saw Gilbert Harding without realising he was gay as well as grumpy, Jimmy Edwards without knowing he was gay and living with an Australian transvestite and Pat Kirkwood without knowing she was soon to be having a hot affair with Prince Philip.

Television (and BBC Radio) was deeply paternalistic and patronising. It wanted to educate us for our own good. A certain amount of that was fine but in the end it drove us from trashy soap operas like *The Grove Family* and *Dixon of Dock Green* to popular music and the doubtful delights of American culture. There was music on television and radio including the whole of Radio Luxemburg and the serious stuff on the Third Programme. There was plenty of popular music — remember Anne Shelton and Alma Cogan? (fine big strapping girls). England had stars such as Frankie Vaughan and Donald Peers and there were constant attempts to find something new, the favourite being a 'relaxed' approach ('I saw Esau'). As time went by we saw more and more American programmes — *The Perry Como Show*, *I Love Lucy* and *Dragnet*. Sometime in the '50s my idea of 'America' moved from New York to California, from the temperature variations of *Some Like it Hot* to the constant sunshine of *I Love Lucy*.

We were all still a bit in love with America from the wartime contact and we heard marvellous accounts of the way things were over there — big houses, plenty of room, warmth, big cars and supermarkets! Sometime during the '50s America sent us something called rock 'n roll: Bill Haley and the Comets sang *Rock around the Clock*. Then Guy Mitchell sang *Singing the Blues*. To the children who had thought that pop music consisted of Bing Crosby these were welcome eye-openers. Also welcome, to me at least, were the western, slightly wailing sounds of, for example, Slim Whitman in *I'll take you home again, Kathleen*, or the hit song, *Hang down your head Tom Dooley*. I remember when I was about 14, a girl in the form below mine at school had brought in her record player, as we were starting to call gramophones. This was not forbidden, but only because no-one had got round to forbidding it. She had also bought her record of Tom Dooley and she and someone else were jiving to it in part of one of the classrooms. A very evocative period piece in my memory. We were all enthralled, especially by how slow it was.

Alongside all this ran a culture of Chapel, Sunday School, hymns and folk songs. It wasn't clear at the time which would win out, as they would say today.

The 1950s passed by and such changes as we saw seemed gradual at the time. My cousin Peter left the RAF, qualified as an accountant and got married. He and his new wife, Pam, bought a house in a suburb — a new concept to me. I knew the country and towns and villages and Council estates but not acres of middle-class, owner-occupied semis set near commuter routes into London. But they must have known what they wanted and we were eager to learn about their new world. The kitchen surfaces were covered with formica, a magical new material which was practically heat-proof. There were glass doors which opened between the front room and the dining-room. A neat little garage stood against one side of the house and there was a neat little garden back and front. I was still a little girl and when we stayed in the house the night before the wedding, CWJ and I packed as much confetti as we could into the bed, the drawers etc. But what a contrast that house was to ours, and they would have cereals for breakfast. We now learnt — or I did — of the existence of corn flakes!

Back at home, things were still moving relentlessly ahead. Every week CWJ took the *Farmers Weekly*. I soon grew old enough to read the recipes and funny bits. EMJ took a regrettable magazine, the *Woman's Weekly*. All the aunts and neighbours also took it. Perhaps there wasn't anything else. It was full of the Mills and Boon type of romances (just right for me at about 13), most of them set in this country with only a tentative nibble at European locations such as Portugal or Paris and a few old colonial settings — Africa, the Far East, Australia.

I was never a good reader of comics. I used to have something called *Sunny Stories* by Enid Blyton but there was some sort of argument about it at home. 'All right', I said, 'I don't want it any more.' So it was cancelled. Later I hated *Girl* but the death-knell for that was that my headmistress strongly approved of it. I couldn't cancel it quickly enough. But I was a great reader of books — anything from Enid Blyton to Frank Richards to Sir Walter Scott.

Most of the books were very dated, some genuinely coming from the 1930s and even earlier and some being set in a sort of never-never land in the school story period when everyone had a cook and a maid, children ate egg sandwiches and sausages and drank ginger beer and went everywhere by cycle, except for train journeys to and from school. Most implausible of all, it was always warm enough for them to camp out in the Easter holidays. So the retro influence of books was on one side, and on the other, television and popular music were looking ahead. So were clothes: one summer skirts began to stick out and we all had to have stiffened petticoats to support them and plastic 'popper' beads. I wore my hair in long plaits till I was about 15 when I gave way and had it cut. Aunts kept telling me I should use make-up, but I hated all that stuff.

At home it was seen as my 'job' to do well at school work and get ready to go to university. I had been working hard, and I mean really hard. I collected a range of 'O' levels as we called them then, and moved from Hill House to Ludlow High School. There I passed some 'A' levels and got a place at London University. So I was lucky enough to be a student and then work for a time in London in the 1960s.

But the real delight was having 'home' in the background. When I was 19, CWJ and EMJ bought me a car. They justified the cost carefully — how many journeys had they had to make to London, or to Worcester or Shrewsbury stations to pick me up? But CWJ's real motivation was: 'I didn't have a car that would go fast until I was too old to appreciate it. She shan't be the same!' EMJ was more concerned with safety after we'd seen a Rolls and a Mini collide. The Mini spread itself everywhere and the Rolls was hardly scratched or dented. 'I didn't want you to have a mini'. So an Austin 1100 was bought and I had the freedom of the road as well as everything else. The pull of home was still strong and I spent a lot of time there, always happy to be back inside the county boundary.

One morning in 1954 CWJ got up early as usual to do the milking. As he was coming back to the dairy, he fell and dropped the buckets, then got up and finished the milking. When he came indoors, he said he didn't feel well, and the doctor was called. He came at once, and CWJ was sent to bed. I was never sure whether what he called 'my seizure' was a cerebral thrombosis or a heart attack. We only knew that other hard-working farmers of a similar age had similar attacks, and we were lucky to keep him.

Yet CWJ and EMJ continued to think about their farm. With the advice of George Davies, the auctioneer in Ludlow, CWJ looked at renting Ludford, but decided it was too big and too smart. After all, we were just country people, not farming aristocracy. At about this time, when he was already past 60, and well-settled at Aldon, the tenancy of Wilmington became available, the landlord of which was Sir Offley Wakeman, the good old friend of Rorrington days. Wilmington was a big, smart Victorian farm — at least, that's how it seemed to EMJ when her grandparents and Uncle Richard had it, and worked it with superb Shire horses.

So CWJ braced himself to do something more for his love — and after all, a few years at Wilmington would be a splendid end to their career. He rang up to arrange a visit. A family of EMJ's cousins lived there, Winnie Watkin and her brothers. Winnie answered the phone. 'I don't mind you coming here, but I'm not having that wife of yours in this house' was her stunning reply. To us, he laughed and said it was because she used to be sweet on him, but there was no question of going there on those terms. So the three of us went, but only looked round outside: we didn't like it much. It was dirty and run down, not at all the smart place EMJ remembered, and the pens for fattening stock were right outside the house. Not that I had much say in the decision, as I was going away to university.

A tender form was filled in, but how pleased we were when we found that CWJ had forgotten to post it in time for the deadline, and how happy he was when he realised we were really pleased. Now we could stop at home and be comfortable.

The comfort only lasted for a short time. CWJ was ill and was in hospital twice in the '60s, once with an arthritic hip and once with

Corndon Hill from Hyssington churchyard

cancer, so they retired and moved. Once he retired, he looked at re-adjusting the balance of work in the house, and I'm proud to say that, before feminism hit home, he started to do his own washing. They had a little time alone together while I was a student and they made new friends. They found the ideal site, in Montgomery, for their dream home, but he died, leaving her to build and live in the dream home without him. It was nice too — a roomy 1970s bungalow with a marvellous view of Corndon at the back and Montgomery Castle at the front.

When he died aged 72, she could only say 'We've never been apart for 40 years.' In 1985 EMJ died of cancer too, saying 'It's been a good life.'

Postscript

Let's imagine we're looking at the scenery in the late springtime in the '30s. Everything is turning green in front of us — fields and hedges — but the hilltops are still bare. Lower down the grass is uneven and lumpy — the ground hasn't been drained. The meadow-land hasn't been ploughed for generations, and lots of wild flowers are growing there at the right time, including cowslips and early purple orchids. Later there will be mushrooms. Fields which will hold stock must have good fences and a water-supply — a pool or a stream. Otherwise they simply can't be used for livestock.

There are more and smaller fields than there are today, and the hedges and gates are in a bad condition: the Depression means that no landlord or farmer can afford to maintain them properly. Hedges that have been brushed or pleached have been done a bit at a time by hand, not by modern mechanised flails. Around every farm, village and town, there are small patches of accommodation land. Transport and delivery of goods is by horse, and horses need paddocks to graze in, near the farm or shop where they work. Early in the morning some wretched boy will be sent out to bring the horse in, and catching it will not always be easy.

Most of the farms and cottages are rented, not owner-occupied, so any paintwork on doors and windows will be the same colour. You got what the landlord's foreman chose. Repairs take a long time, and investment in improvements is low. Cottages are small and in poor condition, but the gardens round them are in good heart and carefully tended.

In the old days (Victorian 'high farming' times) there were good dry roadways to the farmhouses, and some attempts at smartness in planting a garden, but that has gone now, and the farms are muddy unless the weather is dry, when they are dusty.

At this time of year the ploughing is over, but it was only finished in spring, and spring-sown corn will not be ready for harvest until September. Lambing is just about over too. The ewes, a mix of different breeds, were doing really well if they averaged a lamb-and-a-half each. There were no specialised lambing sheds, although they might have had a bit of shelter around or even in some of the farm buildings, with pens made from bales of hay or straw. Then back out to the fields, where they look very thinly scattered in comparison with today's huge flocks.

The cows are a mixed lot too — both roan and blue Ayrshire pattern, some Hereford type, some looking like Friesians, but the Channel Island types being too delicate for our conditions, and other continental breeds like Charolais and Limousin not heard of. There is a dairy herd at every farm we can see, but all the cattle have thick coats from being outside a lot in winter. There aren't many young cattle being reared for beef. Replacement milkers are reared, but young bull calves are sold off as soon as possible. There is little market for beef, and what are worn-out milkers for anyway? Near some of the big farms a bull, if he is of a placid breed, may be seen enjoying being outside. He has to work hard for his living, being used (in exchange for money) to impregnate the cows whose owner cannot afford to keep a bull.

There are no tractors in the scene before us, but quite a few cart-horses helping with the never-ending job of muck-spreading. Implements lie around the farms, but the most commonly used seems to be the fork or shovel. A little later it will be the hoe, as farm-workers and piece-workers together get on with hoeing root crops. The farm must have an engine somewhere, because there is no jinney-ring. An engine has a lot of uses — principally for running the milking-machine, for chopping roots, shearing and other jobs. Some engine is necessary if corn is to be crushed for feed for cattle. You can see where the threshing-machine stands when it visits for a few days at a time to fill the storage areas with grain from the stacks of sheaves gathered at harvest. Everything is still of the size a man can carry, or a woman at harvest-time. So hay is loose, corn comes in sheaves, and is bagged into 1cwt sacks and baled into small bales at threshing-time.

The countrymen we can see are wearing a uniform of thick whitish-brown corduroy trousers and heavy boots, or perhaps Wellington boots, plus any old clothes they can find. If it's wet, they may be wearing an old corn sack split down one side to make a hood-and-cape in one. The days of buying working sweaters and overalls, instead of wearing out old clothes, have not yet arrived. Women aren't much to be seen out of doors, except for a farmer's wife feeding the poultry, or another in a trap on the way to market.

The roads carry little traffic — a few cars and small lorries, some horse-drawn vehicles, a lot of bicycles, and quite a few pedestrians, who make use of paths as shortcuts. Road surfaces are being improved, but the lanes are free of tarmac and have a strip of green up the middle, sometimes with the marks to show where a single cyclist, such as the postman, rides every morning.

As the day moves on to evening, a few — very few — weak lights show. There is no danger of a few oil lanterns causing 'light pollution' so we have a clear view of Jack and his Wagon, and the Milky Way.

Some Shropshire Gardens Revisited
by Barbara & Alan Palmer

Written by two dedicated plant and garden lovers, this describes 50 gardens scattered across Shropshire, most of which are open to the public at various times during the year. The book is crammed with information, observation and pictures that includes: the history and development of each garden; what there is to see; unusual plants and trees; practical advice on the care of plants; ideas for garden design and planting tips. Alan and Barbara Palmer have lived in Shropshire most of their lives making and nurturing three gardens, all of which are open under the National Gardens Scheme.

ISBN: 1 904396 34 8 (978 1 904396 34 5)
Paperback, 128 pages 130 colour photographs   Price £9.95

A Matter of Life and Death.
The Secrets of Shrewsbury Cemetery
by Peter Francis

Shrewsbury Cemetery is a delightful open space in which to wander and, given time, to discover the graves of many who played a role — for better or worse — in the history of the town, and sometimes on a much broader stage. Present are many of Shrewsbury's mayors, several victims of the two world wars including German and Italian PoWs, and two old soldiers who fought in the historic Charge of the Heavy Brigade in the Crimean War.

There are those who drowned in the River Severn, others killed in rail crashes, fires or freak events. Those commemorated include the locally well known, such as Arthur Rowley, Mary Webb and Hilda Murrell, as well as many whose stories and achievements are long forgotten — doctors, missionaries, ministers, business leaders, footballers, refugees and many more.

Peter Francis has lived most of his life in the Stiperstones area as have his ancestors for several hundred years. A life-long passion for local history has led to numerous magazine articles, talks and guided tours.

ISBN 1 904396 58 5 (978 1 904396 58 1)
Paperback, 144 pages with 64 photographs and illustrations   Price £9.95

Also from Logaston Press

Cinderallas & Packhorses:
A History of the Shropshire Magistracy
Edited by David J. Cox *and* Barry S. Godfrey

This book provides a very readable and clear picture as to how the early forerunners of Justices of the Peace came about during the reigns of Richard I, Edward I and Edward II, and developed over time. The duties that Justices of the Peace have had to perform have been varied and encompass collecting rates for the repair of bridges, trying those accused of felony and trespass, the regulation of wages and prices, the maintenance of gaols and Houses of Correction, the suppression of disorderly houses, appointment of parish constables, tracing and prosecuting recusants, controlling of riots, fining women deemed to be living idly, judging those killing game, licensing of alehouses, dealing with vagrancy, administration of Poor relief, ensuring the maintenance of a bastard child by its alleged father, ordering people to the stocks or whipping post, dealing with those who uttered a profane oath, judging those who worked on a Sunday, administration of the county rate, the regulation of Turnpike Trusts, supervising the administration of asylums, the formation of police forces and, most recently, dealing with many motoring offences — and that is not a definitive list. These and other duties are all covered. The book successfully explains what was happening nationally, as well as the concerns, issues, and some of the cases that were being dealt with locally. It ends by raising the issues that face the Magistracy today, not least in terms of the professionalisation of the service, and the tension between use of local knowledge and a desire by central government for blanket uniformity.

ISBN: 1 904396 45 3 (978 1 904396 45 1)
Paperback, 112 pages, 30 illustrations   Price £9.95

Also from Logaston Press

The Churches of Shropshire & their Treasures
by John Leonard

This book explores 320 parish churches of Shropshire, half of them medieval. Chapters guide the reader through changing architectural styles, from Anglo-Saxon origins to the 21st century and then detail the treasures of the churches, including towers and spires, porches roofs, sculpture, fonts, memorials and monuments, stained glass, rood-screens, pulpits, pews and chancel furnishings. The county is then divided into geographical areas, with descriptions of all the individual churches in each area.

John Leonard is a retired consultant physician who lives in Shropshire and has written numerous books on churches.

ISBN 1 904396 19 4 (978 1 904396 19 2)
336 pages, over 530 illustrations   Price £12.95

The Folklore of Shropshire
by Roy Palmer

Shropshire's folklore is presented in a series of themed chapters that encompass landscape, buildings, beliefs, work, seasons, people, music and drama. In the eleven chapters the county's rich store of folklore unfolds in a way that allows you to dip into what most intrigues, or to read from start to finish. Here are stories of mark stones, stone circles, giants, tunnels, dragons, rivers, meres, pools, hills, church sites changed by the devil, vengeful spirits, bull and bear baiting, cockfighting, fairs, herbal remedies and those which involve peculiar activities, minstrels, histriones, waits, charmers and 'cunning folk', ghosts, witches, bountiful cows, of characters such as the early saints, Caratacus, Edric the Wild, Humphrey Kynaston, Jack Mytton and even recent folklore surrounding Hilda Murrell, of tales of the Civil War and of Hopton Quarter, of celebrations and customs surrounding Christian festivals along with the likes of 'burning the mawkin', 'tin panning' and wife selling, of rhymes that link villages, ballads that tell of events in the county's past, of folk plays and mummers — to mention just some of what is included.

ISBN 1 904396 16 X (978 1 904396 16 1)
Paperback, 320 pages, over 250 illustrations   Price £12.95